ISBN 978-0-266-83395-6
PIBN 10896349

This book is a reproduction of an important historical work. Forgotten Books uses
state-of-the-art technology to digitally reconstruct the work, preserving the original format
whilst repairing imperfections present in the aged copy. In rare cases, an imperfection in
the original, such as a blemish or missing page, may be replicated in our edition. We do,
however, repair the vast majority of imperfections successfully; any imperfections that
remain are intentionally left to preserve the state of such historical works.

FORTY-THIRD

ANNUAL REPORT

OF THE

HAWAIIAN

Mission Children's Society,

PRESENTED JUNE 1, 1895,

WITH THE

CONSTITUTION AND BY-LAWS

AND

Full * List * of * Members.

HONOLULU:

PRESS PUBLISHING COMPANY PRINT.

1895.

OFFICERS FOR 1894-5.

REV. O. P. EMERSON, PRESIDENT.

W. W. HALL, VICE-PRESIDENT.

W. L. HOWARD, RECORDING SECRETARY.

MRS. L. B. COAN, CORRESPONDING SECRETARY.

HON. W. F. FREAR, TREASURER.

F. A. HOSMER AND MISS M. A. CHAMBERLAIN,
ELECTIVE MEMBERS OF THE BOARD.

OFFICERS FOR 1895-6.

PROF. THEODORE RICHARDS, PRESIDENT.

J. S. EMERSON, VICE-PRESIDENT.

W. L. HOWARD, RECORDING SECRETARY.

MRS. L. B. COAN, CORRESPONDING SECRETARY.

REV. O. H. GULICK, TREASURER.

REV. O. P. EMERSON AND MRS. O. H. GULICK,
ELECTIVE MEMBERS OF THE BOARD.

MINUTES OF THE ANNUAL MEETING,
HELD JUNE 1, 1895.

The annual meeting of the Hawaiian Mission Children's Society was held Saturday, June 1, 1895, at the residence of Mr. J. B. Atherton. The meeting was opened with prayer, led by Rev. H. Bingham. D.D.

Twenty-seven members were present—the president, Rev. O. P. Emerson, occupying the chair.

Minutes of meeting of May 4, 1895, were read and approved.

The minutes of the meeting of the Board of Managers of May 18 and June 1, were read and accepted.

The following were made eligible to membership, upon payment of dues, as recommended by the Board:

Mr. C. Frasher, Rev. and Mrs. J. Leadingham, and Miss Grace Richards.

The collection was now taken, amounting to $9.75, after which the report of the recording secretary for the year was read, and ordered printed in the Annual Report.

The report of the corresponding secretary was next read, and also ordered printed in the Annual Report of the Society.

The treasurer gave a verbal report, stating that the $2250, as appropriated at the beginning of the year, had been raised and paid out as ordered, "leaving him penniless." It was voted that when the report was completed and audited by the vice-president, it be printed with the others in the Annual Report.

The president now stated that the election of officers for the coming year was in order.

Judge W. F. Frear was nominated and elected president, but upon Mrs. Frear stating that Judge Frear was unable to serve, his resignation was accepted.

Chief Justice A. F. Judd was nominated, but refused on account of arduous duties and the distance
of his home from the center of the town.

Another nomination for president was referred to
the Board of Managers.

The following officers were elected as recommended
by the Board :

Vice-President, Mr. J. S. Emerson ; recording secretary, W. L. Howard ; corresponding secretary, Mrs.
L. B. Coan ; treasurer, Rev. O. H. Gulick ; elective
members of the Board of Managers, Rev. O P.
Emerson and Mrs. O. H. Gulick.

Mrs W. F. Frear was nominated for an elective
member of the Board, but was obliged to refuse, and
Mrs Gulick was elected.

The appropriations, as recommended by the Board,
were carried as follows :

For support of teachers in Kawaiahao Seminary........$200 00
For support of pupils in Kawaiahao Seminary....... .. 200 00
For support of pupils in East Maui Female Seminary ... 200 00
For support of pupils in Kohala Girls' School.......... 200 00
For support of pupils in Hilo Boys' Boarding School... 200 00
For Kauai Industrial School......................... 200 00
For aid to schools of Chinese Mission................ 200 00
For aid to schools of Portuguese Mission.... .. .. 200 00
For aid to Japanese Mission Work..... ....··· 100 00
For Mortlock Teachers 300 00
For Corresponding Secretary........................ 60 00
For publishing Annual Report................... .... 110 00
For Contingencies 30 00
                                                    ─────────
     Total. $2200 00

It was voted that the Mortlock teachers be request-
ed to assist the Society in raising the $300 appro-
priated, by sending mats, fans, shells, and other
salable articles to the Society.

Mr. G. P. Castle, who has had charge of the Maile
Wreath papers for many years, was re-elected for the
ensuing year, with the recording secretary as assistant.

The Maile Wreath editors to serve four months, beginning with the July meeting, were elected as follows : Mr. C. J. Lyons, chairman ; Rev. O. H. Gulick, Miss Laura Pires and Mrs. J. H. Higgins. Editors to serve four months, beginning with November, were elected as follows: Prof. T. Richards, chairman ; Miss Nettie Hammond, Mr. W. E. Beckwith and Miss M. A. Brewer.

It was voted that the address of the retiring president be read at the adjourned annual meeting, to be held June 15th at the home of Chief Justice Judd.

At this adjourned meeting Rev. O. H. Gulick was appointed secretary *pro tem.*, in the absence of the recording secretary, W. L. Howard.

Mr. C. Frasher was made eligible to membership upon payment of fee.

The corresponding secretary was authorized to make further additions to her report.

The report of the treasurer was read and accepted. The treasurer was by vote directed to look up the condition and manner of investment of the Bond Fund, and report at the next meeting.

Prof. T. Richards was unanimously elected president for the ensuing year.

The appropriation, "Aid to schools of Portuguese mission," was amended to read, "Aid to Portuguese mission work."

The report of the retiring president, Rev. O. P. Emerson, was now read and listened to with much interest by the members present.

Brief addresses were also made by Rev. Douglas P. Birnie, and Rev. Capt. Walkup, of the schooner *Hiram Bingham.*

Mrs. Judd, Miss Judd and Miss Fleming furnished music for the evening.

W. L. Howard,
Recording Secretary.

REPORT OF RECORDING SECRETARY.

Our meetings during the past year have been one less than usual, on account of the existence of martial law during January, but, including the meeting to-night, the total attendance has been 408, or an average of thirty-seven for the eleven meetings.

Special music selections have been given by Misses Dixon, Axtell, Richards, Burhans, Carrie Castle, Jones, Smith, and the Kamehameha Glee Club.

The Maile Wreath presented some very interesting and valuable talks and essays, among which were the following: "The Mausoleums of India," Mrs. E. B. Maxwell; "The Jews in New York," W. N. Armstrong; "Night-blooming Cereus," Mrs. W. F. Frear; "An Hawaiian Story," Prof. W. D. Alexander; "College Life of Girls," Mrs. W. F. Frear; "Theosophy and Its First Converts," W. R. Castle; "A Visit to the South and Hampton Institute," Miss M. A. Brewer; "The Alleged Neglect of Industrial Training by the Missionary Fathers," Prof. W. D. Alexander; "The Alleged Refusal of the Missionary Sons to Enter into the Work of Their Fathers," Rev. S. E. Bishop; "Incidents of Missionary Labor in Hawaii," Rev. S. E. Bishop; "Battle of the Roses," Miss A. E. Judd; "My Trip to Hualalai," A. W. Crockett; "Incidents of Portuguese Life," Mrs. A. V. Soares; "The Physiology of the Tenement House," Rev. Kenneth Duncan; "Helen's Emergency," Mrs. W. F. Frear; Egoism and Altruism," Mrs. J. M. Whitney; "A Lullaby" (poetry), Mrs. W. F. Frear; "Reminiscences of Mr. Edward Bailey During the Time of Kamehameha III" (read by Mrs. Frear); "The New, Old Testament," Rev Kenneth Duncan.

Many of the subjects in the above list were treated in a manner which makes them of value historically.

It has been suggested that the volumes of the Maile Wreath be indexed and placed in the rooms of the Historical Society.

The following have acted as editors of the Maile Wreath during the year: Mrs. A. B. Lyons, Mrs. W. F. Frear, W. N. Armstrong, Dr. N. B. Emerson, Mrs. L. B. Coan, Rev. S. E. Bishop, Prof. W. D. Alexander, Miss Agnes Judd, Mrs. J. M. Whitney, Mrs. A. B. Soares, A. W. Crockett and Rev. Kenneth Duncan.

In order to make it easier for members to serve upon the Maile Wreath committee, it has been thought best to nominate more than one month in advance, and at the annual meeting a committee was also nominated to serve four months, beginning in November.

Twenty-eight new members have been received during the year.

HONORARY MEMBERS.—Dr. and Mrs. Rife, Rev. and Mrs. Price, Rev. R. G. Hutchins.

For the Annual and Life Members added this year, see the Treasurer's Report.

The good attendance at the meetings during the year is an index that the design of the society to " cherish and promote union amongst its members," is meeting with a happy fulfilment and the gratifying increase in membership makes a wider field " to cultivate an active missionary spirit, stir up our members to do good work, and, more especially, to assist in the support of Christian missions."

Respectfully submitted,

W. L. HOWARD,
Recording Secretary

ANNUAL REPORT OF CORRESPONDING SECRETARY.

When the *Morning Star* sailed away from our waters last July, bound on her annual voyage to Micronesia, she bore a precious cargo. There were five recruits for the mission field : Mr. and Mrs. Price, mature in experience, having been several years missionaries in China ; Dr. and Mrs. Rife (ardent, enthusiastic "Volunteers"), full of happy anticipations for their work ; and Miss Crosby, whose restored health she gladly re-consecrated to the Master's use. Mrs. Garland, the captain's special mate, but missionary always wherever she may be, went as passenger. With these there were, also, Helen Price, a little girl of nine summers, and wee Dorothy Garland.

Although the *Star* is always laden with blessings, it seemed this time that her freight was richer than ever. Scriptures, hymn books, school books in five languages, live stock, plants, bees, boxes and bundles galore, these all were going as proofs of thoughtful deeds for needy ones. How gladly, we heard, in course of time, of their safe arrival at their respective stations —Dr. and Mrs. Rife and Miss Crosby at Kusaie, Mr. and Mrs. Price at Ruk. Now that our little ship has returned to us, how many interesting details we have of the welfare and work of

OUR MICRONESIAN COUSINS.

Of Mr. Walkup we learn that, during 1894, his itinerating tours in his gasoline craft, the *Hiram Bingham*, had required seventy-two anchorings ; that he had prepared by mineograph 9000 leaves of international Sunday school lessons, scattering these with much seed, also, of the spoken word. At some of the islands dancing and drunkenness were holding the poor natives in the bondage of Satan ; on other islands there were drouth, poverty and hunger. At Tapeteuea he attended the funeral of a good old deacon, whom he calls "a walking Bible," as he could repeat not only chapters but books of the New Testament. At Apaiang the king had signed a bill, sent in by his cabinet, prohibiting the use of tobacco, and dancing also, as it had "so upset things." At Maiana the king tells the people that "dancing was locked out." At Banaba, "away off on the ocean," two vessels had during the year been buying shark-fins. Some of the poverty stricken people, refusing tobacco in trade, had each secured a half-dollar for the fins, but had no more money to buy Bibles with. Mr. Walkup had helped them to the other half, "and Banaba," he says, "is richer than if several showers had reached them." Summing up statistics, he tells us that there has been received from sale of scriptures $634.75, from other books, $271.89, while "missionary collections" amounted to $389.25, a total of $1295.89 for a people than whom there are few on earth more impecunious. Let our sympathy and our aid go to Mr. Walkup. Without a home other than his little boat, without a companion of his own race, without one intelligent seaman to bear the heavy strain of care that must come on one navigating a sometimes disabled and leaking boat, amidst dangers of wind and tide and current, he surely needs encouragement and some coöperation.

Rev. Mr. Channon and Miss Hoppin give very interesting accounts of their touring with their pupils through the Gilbert group on the *Morning Star*. The story she tells of a brave girl who resisted temptation and persecution at the hands of her relatives, that she might not return to heathenism, suffices to assure us that labor is not in vain in rescuing these children ot the isles.

Mrs. Channon's busy days had been exchanged for

a period of quiet rest, made necessary by illness and prostration from overwork. Of Mrs. Price's severe illness we learn with regret, but give thanks to the gracious Healer that health was restored.

Miss Palmer, Miss Foss and Miss Kinney remain at their posts, doing faithful work. Ruk's bit of sunshine, as Mrs. Logan called Miss Abell, came to Honolulu by advice of the mission, wisely to forestall breaking down.

At "Gilbertinia" brains and pens have been busy. Mrs. Bingham has revised and had published a new edition of her Gilbert Islands arithmetic.

Dr. Bingham has prepared and put through the press a Bible dictionary, finely illustrated with cuts procured from the American Tract Society. To this there is also added a concordance, and the next trip of the *Star* will take these new treasures to the waiting people.

COUSINS IN JAPAN.

We have been favored by Rev. O. H. Gulick with the following :

"T. W. Gulick and wife are located as missionaries of the Christian Alliance, at Miyoshi, where they are fully and deeply engaged in evangelistic work. Their son Walter is teaching in Wisconsin. Miss Julia Ann E. is doing valiant touring work in different cities of the large Southern island of Kyushu. She spends weeks, yes months, first in one city, and then in another, accompanied by a Japanese Christian woman helper; sometimes stopping at Japanese hotels, at other times hiring a little abode and keeping house. When thus located she furnishes herself with bedstead, chairs and table, but when on the move, as she often is for weeks, she is destitute of even these three foundation requisites of Western civilization."

Mr. Gulick gives also an extract from a letter from his nephew, Sidney S.

"The complete change of front of the army officials on the question of admitting Christian literature in the army is almost worthy of being placed among the miracles of history. Rev. H. Loomis has already distributed about 70,000 copies of the gospels, and 1,300 Testaments to the officers. I heard yesterday that the Emperor had heard of the Bible distribution and had asked for and received a copy of the Testament and that he is studying it daily." Mr. Gulick adds: "The outcome of the war is sure to be that the word of God as revealed in the Book will be more fully than ever before proclaimed in the three great Asiatic nations involved. Now is the time to pray that the hearts of our cousins and our missionaries in the Orient faint not."

We have received from Miss Searle acknowledgment of Reports sent her. She writes: "I never felt as if I quite legitimately belonged to the Cousins' Society until a cousin of mine married Hattie Gulick, though I have felt a special interest in every thing connected with the islands since childhood." Miss Searle has been for eleven years connected with the Kobe Girls' School, which they are beginning to call "Kobe College."

Miss McCully writes: "The terrible warfare which has been going on between Japan and China is, of course, an absorbing topic, but the exciting scenes are distant, and life here in Tokyo moves on much in the old manner, except that more troops are met in the city, on their way from one point to another; and in celebration of victories there have been great demonstrations, but in this immense city all these things may take place and leave the majority of people quite undisturbed. I go a long distance in my jinrikisha to an evening school with never a thought of fear. The school is under the auspices of the Y. M. C. A. I have given several hours a week there for over two years."

Of the work of our cousins Wm. H. and Alice Gordon Gulick in Spain we continue to receive cheering reports. In "The International Institute for Girls" at San Sebastien, of which they are the principals, "religious instruction is given daily in graded classes, and a student is expected to review the whole Bible during the course. The Bible is kept in the front among all the books that in this school are to be studied daily and systematically." The curriculum of study compares favorably with those of Eastern colleges, and it is pursued in Spanish, French and English, books in these tongues being used with nearly equal ease and profit by the girls.

Mr Gulick writes: "I little thought when I drew out your letter and the Report to be soon answered, and put them in sight before me, so that they should not be overlooked, such sad news should occur to draw out our feelings so tenderly toward members of our cousin band so suddenly called to suffer such bitter grief. Charles Carter cut down, shot down in the prime of life and with a brilliant future before him. And Henry Castle swallowed up by the waters, with his daughter Dorothy, and not so far away from here! How sad, how very sad. But God is the loving father of us all, and does he not do all things well?"

CORRESPONDENCE IN THE STATES.

Our last year's plea for more help in this line has met with pleasing response. Several delightful communications have been addressed to the Society; more have come to the Secretary as personal favors. Almost without exception the letters have contained the kindest assurances of appreciation of the Annual

Reports, and of intense sympathy in our national struggles.

One of earliest date was from Capt. C. A. Colcord who writes: " I have very pleasant memories of the few years I spent in the Islands, and it has been a great pleasure many times, when argument ran high about your government, and criticisms were severe, to be able to talk understandingly, not only of the cause, but of the people representing each side. Mine has been an easy and convincing victory, from being able to state facts, and contradict a lot of newspaper talk which had no foundation." Of his father, formerly Captain of the " Morning Star," he tells us that he is leader of a Bible class of two hundred members, mostly young men. This is in the Bethesda Sunday School in New York. His sister, Mrs. H. O. Appleby, had met with a sad bereavement in the loss of her son. He writes: " I was thinking if the letters to the Corresponding Sectetary were of so much interest to us, possibly I might help to make it interesting for others, by sending a word of cheer, and letting them know that in their good work my heart was with them, and purse, (which is more to the point) so far as my diversified interests along this line will allow. So I herein enclose twenty dollars, with the wish that I could make it ten times that amount. Please consider it an offering from Capt. and Mrs. C. A. Colcord. How often we prove that saying of the Master, 'more blessed to give than to receive,' and I think the more we do for Him, the better it grows all the way along."

Dr. Lucy M. Ingersoll writes: " I have never forgotten nor ceased to appreciate the honor you did me in admitting me as a member of your circle of Cousins in' 1887. For a long time I have wanted much to tell you of the absorbing interest with which I have watched, from afar, the magnificent struggle you have been engaged in during the past two years. How much I honor you for the course you have pursued in spite of all obstacles. We feel a great admiration for the wisdom, quiet power, good judgment and executive ability of your Republic. I hope the day is not very distant when true hearted Americans can give you a hearty welcome into our sisterhood of States. Honolulu is the dearest place in the world to me. I am there in spirit much of the time."

Mrs. Merritt writes of a home-missionary enterprise, undertaken by the church of which Mr. Merritt is pastor. Fifteen miles from them was a settlement, where, within a radius of two miles and a half, were more than a hundred children who had never seen a minister, many of them had never heard a prayer. Thither went Mr. and Mrs. Merritt for a week of services. "I thought I was a good walker," writes Mrs. Merritt, "but I had hard work to keep up with the women who tramped the roughest trails I ever dreamed of, through the darkness and the mud, to hear the gospel." So plainly did their church seem to hear the Lord say, "These are my children, will you care for them?" That on their knees before Him they answered, "Yes, Lord, we'll undertake it."

Of Rev. Thos. L. Gulick we learn that he has been Representative Secretary of the American McCall Association, and that at a meeting of that Society held in Pittsfield, he gave a strong address on "The Reason why those who desire the Advancement of Civil Liberty should labor for the evangelization of France."

A few lines from Mrs. Luella (Andrews) Kilborne assure us of a desire to aid us if she could. She says: "I sometimes wish that we might all go back to my native land. I dream of it only as it used to be, and when I read of the boys and girls who have grown into manhood and womanhood, the former acting as statesmen. I know not whether to weep or rejoice that the dear old associations are broken up."

To Mrs. Fanny (Andrews) Shepherd the *Lima Kokua* Society of Kawaiahao Seminary sent five dollars, to be used in her mission work as she thought best. It is to be applied to "a school for the poorest of the poor, begun because the mothers begged that their children might not grow up in ignorance, but be able to read God's Word and learn the way of life. The poverty of this people is something terrible; 'hard times' are always present Five dollars will go a great ways here for any charity object."

Mrs. Shepherd speaks of their pleasant visit in America, of Dr. Shepherd's improved health, of their safe journey to Turkey, and of their being met by hundreds of people, who came out as they neared the city (Aintab) to welcome them. Her own health is so poor that she is not able to do what she wishes she could.

Mrs. Mary Clement Leavitt spent the winter for health's sake in Vera Cruz, Mexico. " I have not been at uninterruptedly 'tolerably well, thank you,' as I was last winter," she writes, February 23, "threatened with pneumonia, with cough left behind—but nearly gone, I hope. I do not feel pulled down nor aged now, though I did till within a month. I have had every evening entirely alone since November 9, and but very little speech or sight of anybody at other times. Except for my little Sunday school class, I have not had six hours' talk with any and all, counting in the words with my Spanish servant—no indeed, nor half of six hours. I have not had an unhappy moment, but trust I shall never be so alone again."

Miss Helen Norton writes : " Though I have been very busy, it seems to me I have given more time to explaining the situation in Hawaii, defending its defenders, contradicting sensational and false reports, calling attention to the importance of so small a portion of the earth's surface to the United States, than to any other subject whatever. Accept best wishes for every cousin in the Society. I always feel rich when I count my cousins."

A brief note has been received from **Mrs. McCully** (now Mrs. Higgins), asking for correction of the mistake in giving the initial of a middle name to the late Judge McCully. At the time of her writing she expected to turn her face homeward in about two weeks. Her plans were afterwards changed, and her coming will be later. We extend congratulations and best wishes to Mrs. Higgins in her new relation.

. "What an era you have passed through," writes Mrs. Waters. "Never before have I so longed to be in Hawaii as since the troubles began. We are only two, but we would have been two warm hearts and four industrious hands wherever needed to support good and clean government."

From Mrs. Church's crowded pages we quote: "We have the *Hawaiian Gazette*, and read it very thoroughly. Dr. B. D. Bond has for several years sent it to us direct from the office, which, having read, we forward to his brother Will. We greatly appreciate the favor. We hope and believe that when the terrible cloud of revolution rolls by the Hawaiian skies will be brighter than ever before. We had hoped the little Republic would be established without bloodshed, that the hopes of the Royalist party would die out, and their leaders would become discouraged and give up without actual rebellion." Of family matters she tells us that Mr. Church is in charge of the Michigan School for the Blind. "He makes all the purchases, teaches two classes, moral science and geometry, supervises the entire establishment, and attends to the thousand and one wants of the pupils and teachers. This takes all his time from 6:30 a.m. to 8:30 p.m. Charlie is stenographer in the office of the assistant superintendent of the Lake Shore & Michigan Southern railroad in Cleveland. Is also Sunday school superintendent of the Plymouth church. He is a great robust-looking young man, full of life and fun.

Albert is studying medicine at Ann Arbor. Louie is still at Oberlin, closing her senior year."

Mrs. C. S. Kittridge writes : " We rejoice you have been brought through your dark and trying days so bravely, and have won such heroic laurels And this has resulted as one of the side issues, that this country has learned more of the Islands, their character and resources, than could have come in many years of ordinary living. How much we all hope that your bright days of prosperity are not far away, and that those enchanting valleys and hillsides may be peopled with frugal and law-abiding citizens. I speak as if your prosperous days were not with you now, yet when I read from your Report of the great number who have been able to travel over the world the past year, and of the heavy contributions your people have given to all good objects, I do not see how you could be called anything but prosperous. Dr. and I went as delegates to the General Church Association at Los Angeles. There we were greatly interested to hear Mr. Frear in his urgent appeals for foreign missions. He quoted Honolulu for its generous giving, and made the statement that the Central Union church gave more yearly than all the churches in the State of California, not even excepting Dr. McLean's church of 1200 members. This produced a ripple of excitement, in which I caught the words, ' Bring it into the Union,' ' Make it a State.' "

OCCASIONS.

We are not yet a State—but we *are* a Republic ! Never brighter sun shone out of the deep blue of our tropic sky than that which looked down on the morning of July 4th, 1894, on the important event transpiring at the steps of the old Iolani Palace. The constitution of the Republic was then promulgated, and Hon. Sanford B. Dole took the president's oath of office for the next six years. A few hours later, what had long been known as " Little Britain," was renamed "Independence Park," and a joyous gathering assembled in its capacious pavillion to celebrate with song and speech the 118th anniversary of American Independence, and Hawaii's new birthday.

On the 12th of December scores of cousins with many friends grouped themselves under umbrageous trees about the foundation walls of " Pauahi Hall" at Punahou, to witness the laying of the corner-stone by President Dole. Then on the 19th December we celebrated Founder's Day at Kamehameha, when its usual program was supplemented by the transfer, from the Trustees of the Girls' School, of its keys to Miss Ida M. Pope, which by her were gracefully accepted. This new school for Hawaiians is spacious and elegant. It would be rare to find in any land one with better appointments. Its cupola, in part enclosed with plate glass, commands a panorama of wondrous beauty.

Closely following these happy incidents came the week of fear and gloom ever memorable in our annals. Those were anxious days and nights when martial law prevailed, when cousins old and young were on duty as guards, rifle in hand, on our streets, or in action on the hill sides and in the valleys, while they sought to put down a rebellion that was rife with plans to fill our hearts and homes with loss and agony. Concerning this epoch allow me to quote the forceful words of L. A. Thurston. "Amid hostile environment, amid opposition, treachery and revolution at home and the depressing effects of continuously hostile influences from abroad, President Dole and his associates, to the best of their limited powers and with all the wisdom with which God has endowed them, are maintaining their outer breastworks of civilization in the Pacific, with a reserve consisting of a handful of professional and business men, mechanics and clerks."

Thank God the breastworks *are maintained.* We believe they will be until buttressed by annexation.

Fortunately martial law, effectively enforced for weeks by the ever vigilant Marshal E. G. Hitchcock, was over before the 23rd of April. On the evening of that day fifty or sixty cousins—all descendants of missionaries, three generations being represented by one family—bearing taro, bananas, sugar cane, cocoanuts, pigs and pigeons, and other "mea aloha," advanced in line, as quietly as mirth would allow, to the residence of Hon. S. B. Dole At the gate they were well nigh challenged by the sentinel, but declaring themselves friends, were allowed to enter. The surprise on the part of our gracious President and his charming wife was complete. The birthday *hookupu* was a perfect success.

A poem, written for the occasion, by Miss M. A. Chamberlain was read by Judge Judd, and afterwards published.

ITEMS.

Our students abroad, on their way to spend last summer's long vacation at home, were cruelly delayed two weeks by the " strikes " that so paralyzed travel and traffic, but they came at last, a joyous company.

Fifteen boys from various colleges, are expected soon for the coming holidays—all with an honorable record of a year's earnest and successful work. Through the kindness of a generous "Cousin," Hiram Bingham Jr., with laurels won for Yale in her late intercollegiate debate with Harvard, hopes to be among them.

During the winter Judge W. F. Frear was confined to his bed eight weeks with slow fever. When able to leave it, by medical advice he went at once to Oakland. We noted with pleasure his marked improvement on his return.

After two years of most patiently endured imprison-ment at Punahou, consequent upon a dreadful fall on Diamond Head, Mrs. Edith Lyons is gladly welcomed by us as we see her again at church or in our homes.

Gleesome Margaret Castle, on a holiday ride with her father, was thrown from her horse and borne home unconscious. Assiduous care of physicians for months, and tenderest nursing by her mother, have been blest to her restoration.

Anxiety for the life of George Carter, long and seriously ill, was added to the grief of his dear relatives while they wept over him who slept in death. Restored in a measure, he returns to dwell in the land of his birth.

Miss Hattie Forbes, with a bloom on her cheeks that shows the benefit of a winter spent in the States, has lately arrived.

Miss Bella Lyons also gained in health during her first and much enjoyed visit of two months at the Coast.

Among tourists hither was Mrs. Mary (Tinker) Harvey, with her husband, Dr. Harvey, of Buffalo. She left the Islands in 1841, at the age of two, and it was with great interest she spent a month here. Her visit was saddened by the news of her mother's death.

When a stranger from abroad bore away his lovely bride, Eleanor Waterhouse, to a home at the East, we could but begrudge him. We are more than complacent now that he brings her back to dwell among us. We value him as Sunday school superintendent of Central Union church, and his wife as assistant superintendent. Mr. Wood was formerly a Y. M. C. A. secretary. Our Honolulu Y. M. C. A. secretary has just secured the remaining prize in Cousin Henry Waterhouse's family, and with his bride is now on an extended wedding tour.

MARRIAGES.

Aug. 21, 1894, at Grinnell, Iowa, Mr. Edgar L. Porter to Miss Lily Field Brewer.

Oct. 6, 1894, Mr. Samuel Kauhane to Sarah H. Martin.

Oct. 31, 1894. at Los Angeles, Cal., Mr. James T. Taylor to Miss Ethel M. Webster.

Nov. 6, 1894, at Chicago, Ill., Mr. Joseph A. Simpson to Miss Helen Julia Kinney.

March 12, 1895, at Charleston, Maine, Rev. John Hamilton Higgins to Mrs. Ellen McCully.

March 12, 1895, at Mt. Carmel, Ill., Dr. Francis A. Lyman to Miss Mary Cecelia Aldrich.

April 2, 1895, at New York, Mr. Edward Lewellyn Pratt to Miss Helen Augusta Dickson.

May 1, 1895, in Honolulu, Mr. David W. Corbett to Miss Mary S. Waterhouse.

BIRTHS.

July 15, 1894, at Kusaie, Hiram Bingham, son to Rev. Mr. and Mrs. I. M. Channon.

Sep. 9, 1894, to Mrs. Helen (Lyman) Greer, a son.

Sep. 26, 1894, Bernice, daughter to Mr. and Mrs. C. A. Brown.

Sep. 28, 1894, Joseph Atherton, son to Mrs. Mary (Atherton) Richards.

Oct 22, 1894, Violet, daughter to Mr. and Mrs. H. C. Austin.

Oct. 22, 1894, Caroline Virginia, daughter to Mr. and Mrs. E. W. Austin.

Nov. 28, 1894, Elinor Henry, daughter to Mr. and Mrs. Henry N. Castle.

Dec. 11, 1894, to Mrs. Helen (Chamberlain) Ives, a daughter.

Jan. 7, 1895, Helen Constance, daughter to Mr. and Mrs. Arthur C. Alexander.

Jan. 17, 1895, Margeret Carter, daughter to Mr. and Mrs. L. A. Thurston.

Jan. 27, 1895, Julia Olmstead, daughter to Mr. and Mrs. W. O. Atwater.

March 20, 1895, Daphne, daughter to Mr. and Mrs. F. W. Damon.

April 10, 1895, Harriet Elizabeth, daughter to Mrs. Sarah L. (Smith) Garland.

May 12, 1895, Arthur Foster, son to Mr. and Mrs. J. A. Gilman.

DEATHS.

As we read the roll of the dead at our last annual meeting, we knew not that two others of our band had just passed into life beyond. For their kindred we mourned, for them we rejoiced when the tidings reached us.

On the 11th of June, 1894, the summons came suddenly for Mrs. Caroline H. Bailey. Yet she had watched long and was ready. She died at Oakland, aged 79 years and 10 months.

June 14, 1894, Mrs Louisa L. Gulick went to her reward. Hers was rare consecration to the Master's service, and He honored her with broad fields of usefulness and made her influence widely felt.

On July 14, 1894, Hon. S. N. Castle, at the age of 83 years 11 months, reached the end of his pilgrimage. For years he was a tower of strength in this community, relied on in civic, business and ecclesiastic relations. His last years were marked by great feebleness, borne with Christian fortitude. At his burial his four sons tenderly laid the remains in the grave. But who in that company of sympathizing friends could foresee what grave awaited one of those bearers ?

At Grinnell, Iowa, Oct. 10, 1894, aged 58, Mrs. Julia M. (Richards) Brewer. It is said by her pastor : " Her life was one of devotion to God, of faithfulness to duty, of sweetness to all." As she came to the hour of release from much bodily suffering, she was able to say: " Though I walk through the valley of the shadow of death I will fear no evil."

At Honolulu, Nov. 22, 1894, Bernice Brown. Scarcely two months on earth, then transplanted to the garden of the Lord.

At Cambridge, Mass., Nov. 30, 1894, Pierre J. Gulick, aged 21. One who knew him well says : "He was loving and lovable, gentle and self-controlled, a conscientious Christian and an earnest student."

In Honolulu, Jan. 3, 1895, at the age of 86 years and 4 months, Mr. Henry Dimond. It must have been a happy new year that brought to Father Dimond the end of mortality and the beginning of immortal-ity ; for infirmity, pain and loneliness—youth renewed, reunion with the companion so recently gone before, and admission to the Saviour's presence.

On the 4th of Jan., 1895, our dear Miss Knight passed also into the bliss of heaven. So much was she with us in her quiet way in the varied activities of life, a comfort and a cheer to all, it has been hard to realize we shall meet her no more on earth.

In the early morning of Jan. 7 a strange, sad word passed through our community: " Charles Carter died at five." Could we believe it ? One so vigorous, in the very prime of manhood and its highest promise, silent in death ! At the first knowledge of an uprising among the royalists, Mr. Carter put himself among the defenders of the government to disperse the gath-ering company of insurgents. Alas ! shot from ambush, a rebel's ball sped on its deadly mission, and our cousin fell. The Lord of Hosts graciously use the sacrifice of the precious life for the country's good.

On the 8th of Jan. came again the angel of death, bringing bereavement to a wide circle of our member-

ship. The aged Father Waterhouse, with quiet trust
and glad hope, heard the call of the messenger and
went hence.

Henry N. Castle was in Germany when news of
the rebellion reached him.   Plans for future work and
study were at once laid aside.   With heart alive for
his country's welfare, and taking his beautiful child,
little Helen Dorothy, with him, he embarked on the
Elbe to return at once to Hawaii.   How hearts were
agonized by the disaster that befell that ship's large
company, overwhelming them with dismay, Jan. 30.
We can never know what last thoughts of home and
heaven filled their breasts as the chill waves of the
North Sea engulfed them.   But we may leave them
in the Father's keeping.   With Charles Carter's name
we enroll that of Henry Castle on the honored list of
martyr patriots.   In his last letter home Mr. Castle
had written that Dorothy was angelic.   Blessed little
one, to be among the angels now.

On the 5th of April, 1895, Mrs. Mary Ellen (Rich-
ardson) Gay was thrown from her carriage and mor-
tally hurt.   The kind, faithful rearing. given her in
girlhood by Mrs. Juliette Cooke bore pleasing fruit in
her careful tending of her own family of seven interesting children.

In Westfield, N.Y., after brief illness, Mrs. Mary T.
Tinker, in her 85th year, went to her crowning. From
1831 to 1840 she was a member of the Hawaiian
Mission.   Her ready acquisition of the native language
and her winning manners made her a valuable and
acceptable worker among the people.

In Hilo, on the 4th of May, 1895, Mrs.. Alameda
(Hitchcock) Moore.

In the spring of 1894, Henry Colcord Appleby.
" Sometime before going hence, he witnessed a good
confession of faith."

" I watched a sail until it dropped from sight
  Over the rounding sea. A gleam of white,
A last far-flashed farewell and, like to thought
Slipt out of mind, it vanished, and was not.

" Yet to the helmsman, standing at the wheel,
  Broad seas still stretched before the gliding keel.
Disaster ?   Change ?   He left no slightest sign,
Nor dreamed he of that dim horizon line.

" So may it be, perchance, when down the tide
  Our dear ones vanish.   Peacefully they glide
On level seas, nor mark the unknown bound.
We call it death—to them 'tis life beyond."

Lydia Bingham Coan.

REPORT OF THE HILO BOYS' BOARDING SCHOOL.

The most encouraging feature of the year has been the deep and prevalent spiritual awakening among the pupils. A large number of the scholars are profess-ing christians, members of Haili church, but we all need reviving, and this has been a year of constant renewel of faith in God and his law.   From four dif-ferent sources have we been supplied with Bibles, and so the smallest pupil reads at morning and evening prayers. Early in the year Captain Milsaps visited us, and his talks and method of holding meetings attracted the boys, so their daily meetings have assumed the form of the Army meetings. The officers have been helpful to them in many ways. The interest has not flagged from the first, has even passed over a two-weeks' vacation without diminishing. One boy says, " I know I am a better boy, because the other day I saw a banana and reached out my hand for it, but I thought, that is not mine, wait till meal time ; and I did ; but before this I would have taken it."

The ice machine, which was put in a year ago, has proved a good investment, and has furnished ice to Hilo and shipping customers at the same rates of supply here as in Honolulu.

Our number has remained about the same, as also the teachers. Substitutes have been furnished by Mrs. Terry and Miss Lyman for part of the year.

We have been unusually free from sickness, aside from the epidemic of German measles.

The yield from the fields has been good, and we are using coffee of our own growing.

We wish to express our united thanks as a corps of teachers and as a school, for the financial help given us by your society. We are not richly endowed with money, but often overpowered with opportunities and responsibilities of work for the Master in Hilo.

CASSIE R. TERRY.

REPORT OF THE EAST MAUI FEMALE SEMINARY, MAKAWAO.

But for one standby, our school would have an entirely new faculty this year. Two teachers left in the summer. Miss McLennon returned to the States on account of lost health. Two months later, Miss Hammond left us to teach in Kamehameha School for Girls.

During the fall term we had fewer pupils than usual, but thirteen new ones have come to us this term, bringing us up to the usual number.

The health of our pupils has been excellent; German measles, and indisposition as the result of vaccination, being almost the only ailments.

Our Sunday prayer meeting has been merged into a Christian Endeavor meeting. Not only the members, but others of the girls take part readily in the meetings, and show an interest in them.

Three of our number have united with the church, and three others have expressed a desire to do so. The influence of the girls who are trying to do right is worth much in stimulating others to make the effort also. Two former pupils, who are now teachers and who board here, are a great help in this direction.

The water which comes to us from a spring three miles up the mountain through pipes, which were put in last year, is clear and fresh and abundant. We all feel very grateful for it. The pipes were put in just in season to prevent grave consequencs, for owing to the drought of last summer, the school would have been obliged to close for a time, had it not been for the new pipes. Those who worked so faithfully for, and contributed toward the work, may feel that their labor and money were expended in a wise way.

We desire to express our thanks to the members of the Cousins' Society for their appropriation to our school. Five of our girls, who are daughters of ministers, are thus provided for.

We desire also to thank the Central Union Sabbath school, Mr. H. P. Baldwin, Mr. C. M. Cooke, Mr. A. S. Wilcox, Mr. G. N. Wilcox and others who have contributed to the school. As times are becoming harder and food more scarce, the Hawaiians are not able to pay as much of the tuition of their children as formerly, so aid is very gratefully received.

M. Ida Ziegler.

REPORT OF THE KOHALA GIRLS' SCHOOL.

Our school opened this year with sixty-one members on the roll, but owing to the change of principals in February we lost ten of our largest girls, leaving us now but fifty-one, two thirds of them quite small. We have had one less teacher than our usual number for the past four months, but we have cause for gratitude that the other teachers have all been strong and well, and that we have had no sickness among the children.

There has been a marked spiritual growth among the girls lately, and we are praying that it may not be for a day, but that it will result in a permanent estab-lishment of character. They have a prayer meeting of their own, two evenings in the week, led by different girls, and all taking some part. The influence of these meetings has been boundless.

We are very grateful to your Society and to all other friends who have given us financial aid this year. We ask your prayers that God's blessing may rest upon our school for the coming year.

MARY O. PAULDING.

REPORT OF THE KAUAI INDUSTRIAL SCHOOL.

Under the efficient management of the principal, Miss A. Bruce, late of Kohala Seminary, the school has passed a successful year.

The boys show an increasing interest in their higher studies.

Good progress has been made in the classes under Mr. Broadbent's charge, in blacksmithing and carpen-tering.

The boys seem willing and faithful in their work on the farm, and are acquiring the habit of steady work done cheerfully and as a matter of course.

Hon. G. N. Wilcox has contributed his generous donation of $600 a year, as in the past. Hon. A. S. Wilcox made a contribution of $200. From Mother Rice was received a contribution of $100.

The Hawaiian Mission Children's Society gave $250; and the Central Union Sunday School gave $50, that pays the tuition of two boys. The Board of Education paid us the $500 appropriated by the Government.

Mr. Macfie of Porto Rico, formerly of Kilauea, Kauai, donated an excellent piano to the school. As the result of a concert arranged for through the efforts of Mrs. W. H. Rice, last summer, the teachers are enjoying the use of a fine new phaeton and harness.

Senator Rice, with his usual generosity, has given the use of a number of cows.

Miss M. Lampman has had charge of the primary department, and Miss Emma Blake, a graduate of Makawao Seminary, has made an efficient matron and teacher of the small boys' sewing and laundry classes.

The pupils range in age from 5 to 18 years, and are well and happy.

The friendliness between teacher and scholar makes Malumalu seem more like a large family than a school.

JULIETTE SMITH, Secretary.

REPORT OF KAWAIAHAO SEMINARY, HONOLULU.

There are eight teachers and one hundred and one girls at Kawaiahao Seminary.

The girls are divided into four classes. The three higher divisions have thirty minute recitations from 9 until 12 a.m.

Miss Abigal Aikue has charge of the primary grade and has shown marked ability in teaching the little ones.

We have three dormitories under the care of the school teachers. Each girl must make up her own bed and keep her clothes in order. The small children are cared for by the older girls.

The domestic department has been very satisfactorily managed by Mrs. Emma Mahelona. The food for both girls and t-achers has been well cooked and nicely served. From the sale of bread and cakes we have realized $50.

The teachers each have charge of a sewing class in the afternoon, from 2 until 3:30 o'clock, when the girls are taught plain sewing. In this department we have earned $125.

Most of the girls make their own dresses. The first term there were twelve girls employed in the dress-making department, but this term there have been but eight. While they have been kept very busy with orders, there have been numerous calls for girls to go out and sew. The girls have together earned for themselves $639.40. The highest amount earned by one girl was by Julia Quinn, which amounted to $182.92.

The Seminary is indebted to the dress making de-dartment for over $600.

We wish to express our gratitude to the Cousins' Society for the entire support of four girls, Lucy Leleo, Mary Piekoi, Mary Opeka and Hina Kualapai, and half the support of two others, Leialoha Kaula and Becky Trask. They are all good girls and seem to appreciate what is being done for them. We also thank the Cousins for $200 for teachers' salaries.

We have been cheered and encouraged by the many ways you have shown an interest in our work at the Seminary.   FLORENCE ALICE PERROTT.

REPORT OF CHINESE MISSION SCHOOLS.

Most gratefully would we of the Chinese Mission acknowledge the continued aid given by the Cousins'

Society to a most important branch of our work. During the past year the work in our different schools has gone forward in a most encouraging manner. Over three hundred young people of ages averaging from 3 or 4 to 23 or 24, have come almost daily under the helpful influences of these schools, in kindergarten, day and boarding schools. Our kindergartens, always interesting, have been the open door into a new and beautiful world for dozens of little celestials, whose lives must be the fairer and better for the up-lift. The Mills Boarding School has been marked by a steady and hopeful growth. Forty-six young men and boys have here found a Christian home during the past year. Most emphatic and earnest are the appeals which this institution makes to all Christian hearts f r support and aid. It is doing a great and far-reaching work and with increased means might influence a still larger number. Will not those able to give, come to our aid in the carrying forward of a work fraught with blessings both to these Islands and to China. Scores of young people in our day and Sabbath schools in Honolulu, Hilo, Kohala and Wailuku are through your aid and that of other friends being formed and fashioned to help onward and upward their country-men into the light of the new day which is, we trust, dawning upon the Chinese. May our Heavenly Father help us to meet aright the great opportunity given to us.

FRANK M. DAMON,
Superintendent of Chinese Mission.

REPORT OF TREASURER OF HAWAIIAN MISSION CHILDREN'S SOCIETY

(For Year Ending May 31st, 1895).

RECEIPTS.

Balance from last account   ..   ..   .. $ 0 00

DONATIONS.

From Hon. H. P. Baldwin	. :.	$ 500 00
Hon. A. S. Wilcox	.	300 00
Rev. E. Bond	.. ..	100.00
Mr. and Mrs. C. M. Cooke..	..	100 00
Hon. S. M. Damon ..	.. ..	50 00
Hon. W. R. Castle ..	.. ..	50 00
Mrs. Cornelia Hall-Jones ..	..	50 00
Mrs. H. E. Cooke ..	.. ..	25 00
Mr. D. Stuart Dodge	.. ..	25 00
Mr. F. J. Lowrie ..	·	25 00
Mrs. A. S. Hartwell	..	25 00
Miss Carrie Bond ..	.. ..	25 00
Rev. and Mrs. O. H. Gulick	..	25 00
Mrs. L. B. Coan ..	.. ..	25 00
Hon. and Mrs. W. F. Frear	..	25 00
Mrs. M. S. Rice ..	.. ..	25 00
Mrs. Geo. P. Castle..	.. ..	25 00
Mr. S. W. Wilcox ..	.. ..	25 00
Prof. A. B. Lyons ..	.. ..	25 00
Hon. and Mrs. W. F. Allen	..	20 00
Capt. C. A. Colcord..	.. ..	20 00
Miss C. D. Castle ..	.. ..	17 00
Kokua Club, per C. H. Cooke, Treas.		15 25
Mrs. A. W. Stetson, Boston	..	11 00
Miss E. B. Lyons ..	.. ..	10 00
Mr. J. S. Emerson ..	.. ..	10 00
Mrs. M. J. Forbes ..	.. ..	10 00
Mr. William J. Forbes	.. ..	10 00
Rev. S. E. Bishop ..	.. ..	10 00
Prof. W. D. Alexander	.. ..	10 00
Pres. F. A. Hosmer ..	. ..	10 00
Mr. and Mrs. Theodore Richards ..		10 00
Mrs. H. C. Coleman ·	.. ..	6 00
Miss Helen S. Judd .	.. ..	5 00

Mrs. Julius Waverly Brown	..		5 00
Miss S. B. Small	.. ..	..	5 00
Miss E. B. Snow	.. ..	..	5 00
Rev. C. M. Hyde, D.D.	..	..	5 00
Rev. O. P. Emerson..	..	..	5 00
Mrs. Sarah Gilman ..	..	..	5 00
Miss Jennie Armstrong	..	..	5 00
Mrs. Maria W. Pogue	..	..	5 00
Donations of one dollar or less	..		21 05

1685 30

LIFE MEMBERSHIP FEES.

For Theodore Richards	..	..	$ 10 00
Robert Shipman Thurston	..	..	10 00
Theodore A. Cooke	.	..	10 00
Miss Isabella Renwick ..	..	..	10 00
Cordelia A. Gilman	..	..	10 00
Joseph Atherton Richards	.	..	10 00
Charles F. Perry	..	..	10 00
Elinor Henry Castle	..	..	10 00
W. L. Howard ..	..	..	10 00
Mrs. Annie E. Atwater..	..	..	10 00
Nathan Schofield	..	..	10 00
Katherine P. Gulick	..	..	10 00
Arthur B. Wood..	..	..	10 00
Juliette Montague Atherton	..	..	10 00
Laura Annis Atherton ..	..	..	10 00
Rev. J. Leadingham	..	..	10 00
Mrs. Anna Rich Leadingham ..	..		10 00

$ 170 00

ANNUAL MEMBERSHIP FEES.

Rev. and Mrs. A. V. Soares, Miss Laura Piies, Miss S.
Brown, Rev. Kenneth J. Duncan, Mr. A. W.
Crocket, Mrs. W. E. Beckwith, Miss Florence A.
Perrott, ... at $1   8 00

MISCELLANEOUS.

Eleven Collections	.. ..	.. ..	130 25
Drawn from the Bond Fund		.. ..	120 00

250 25

$2113 55

DISBURSEMENTS.

Support of Teachers, Kawaiahao Seminary	$200	00
Pupils, Kawaiahao Seminary ..	250	00
East Maui Female Seminary	250	00
Kohala Girls' School ..	250	00
Hilo Boys' Boarding School	250	00
Kauai Industrial School	250	00
Schools of Chinese Mission	250	00
Schools of Portuguese Mission	250	00
Publishing Annual Reports	86	25
Corresponding Secretary	60	00
Contingencies	17	30

—————— $2113 55

E. & O. E.   O. H. GULICK,
Treasurer.

Audited and found correct.

WM. W. HALL,
Vice-President.

ADDRESS OF THE RETIRING PRESIDENT.

———

Our interest in Hawaiian character, especially that of the native pastor and Christian worker, may well lead us back a little to the study of the situation in which they have been placed, to see if with much that has been faultful in their conduct, there are not also some things that are praiseworthy and even heroic.

The members of the native churches show up to-day battered and weak and few, but maybe they have come by their wounds honestly.

There is much in the history of the past thirty years which, if understood, will put their case in a more favorable light, and show, on the part of some of our native brethren, not a little hardihood.

Before we can know the soldier's bravery and excuse the disarray of his equipage, his wounds and lassitude, we must hear the story of his marches and battles.

Let his sufferings be pictured in all their realism— the heat, the cold, the hunger, the forced marches, the fighting, the wounds, the blood—then, aware of these, we will applaud his disarray, and take home to our hearts the appeal of the halting ranks and torn flags.

Undoubtedly the native, be he in the capacity of a pastor or of a deacon and leader in his church, has undergone experiences in which, if anything has been won, it has been from the very clutch of the enemy, and if anything has been lost, it has been in a stub-bornly contested campaign in which he has been fiercely pressed—in marches, cut by ambuscades, and close hand-to-hand fights.

The first crisis which came to the native churches was in the steps taken towards launching them as independent organizations under the charge of native pastors. Worthy as was the intention of this move, which was made in 1863, it is now confessed to have been precipitate.

The history of the last thirty years warrants this conclusion. For, unfortunately, the experiment was tried during a period of storms, and the storms were of unusual severity, and in them the quality of the native christianity was put to an extreme test. It was what the fathers feared, that their beloved successors in the work would be tried overmuch. Gladly would they have had the days of trial postponed. But it was not to be as they wished.

Here are a few figures: There were in 1863 twenty-five churches, under the charge of sixteen American missionaries and four native helpers, with a member-ship of 19,725.

Five years later, in 1868, these twenty-five churches are found to have been divided into fifty, with twelve American missionaries and thirty-five native pastors, the membership having shrunk to 17,377.

Twenty-five years later, in 1888, there are found to have been fifty-seven churches, one American and thirty-two native pastors, and a membership of only 5,235.

These figures indicate a most alarmingly rapid reduction of the Christian force among the Hawaiians, until now, thirty two years later, we learn by the Report of 1895, that there are fifty six churches, all but one of them under the charge of native pastors, with a total membership of only 4,784.

If, in attempting to account for this rapid reduction, we should attribute the cause to the decrease of the native population, we would find that the figures do not bear us out; for while, during the twenty-five years extending from 1865 to 1890, the decrease of population was 30 per cent., the decrease of the church membership was very nearly 70 per cent. There were other causes for the result.

It is undoubtedly true that one underlying cause was the inability of the native pastor to maintain the high standard of effort kept up by the missionary fathers. Yet it is a question if the missionary fathers themselves, had they lived in these later days, under the changed circumstances, could have saved the churches from serious decline—it is a question if they could have kept, through all these later, trying conditions, the high-water mark of the olden time. For there came serious changes into the life of the people, for which the native pastor and Christian were in no wise responsible.

First, there was the change which came by the passing away of the chiefs and the old order of things. Undoubtedly this class of men were of great help to the fathers. They were men of authority in their districts. They were much respected and readily obeyed by the people. What the chiefs commanded to be done, was done. They were, in many cases, men of piety. They stood by the missionary. They exercised in the church a strong, conservative influence.

One of the first Sundays my father spent in his parish at Waialua, he was accompanied by Dr. Judd. The crowd was so great that when they were to be seated it was done simultaneously, by the order of Laanui, the chief. Each was ordered to sit down in his tracks. Misled by the stirring scene of the multitudes before them, the missionaries took it as the sign of the beginning of a work of grace. They afterwards learned that the coming of the people had been by order of the chief. He had told them that the houses of absentees from church would be nailed up. When the missionary expostulated with him for the issuing of such an order, he told the people that though thereafter no force should be used to get them out to church, yet it would be best for them to be actuated by the desire to come.

Now, when we come to the later history of the native churches, to the time when the experiment of the native pastorate was tried, we find no chiefish authority exercised in behalf of their work, for the chief had passed away.

And with the chiefs had also gone the men of the old order, such as had proved themselves sturdy helpers during the first forty years of the mission. These were the men who had been trained under the hand of the missionary—men who were imbued with the spirit of respect and loyalty to the constituted authority, and who upheld the higher ideals of the chiefs and earlier kings, such as Kaahumanu and Kekuanaoa and Kamehamehas III. and IV.

These men stood before the people as the representatives of good government. But when the native pastor came they had mostly passed away

The pastor of the Kaumakapili church told me that when he came to his first parish he was badly handicapped for the lack of just such men. He was left to deal with new material under very changed circumstances.

As one remarked, " The change to the native pastorate took place at the time when implicit obedience to constituted authority was giving place to the preference and personal choice of the individual." And this sense of an enlarged individuality, coming, as it did, at a time when there were most corrupt influences abroad, operated disastrously.

Nor can it be forgotten that this was the time of the increased sectarian activity, marked by the growth of the Anglican influence and the Mormon element. These bodies drew some away from the churches founded by the fathers.

Furthermore, the passing away of the chiefs and their associates in the government, unfortunately for the native pastors, was accompanied by the uprising of the kahuna power.

It was during the premiership and reign of Kamehameha V., just as the native pastor was about entering upon his work, that a very general dealing out of licenses was begun to be made to these irresponsible, evil-minded men.

In the early days the chief exercised a restraining influence over the hula master and the kahuna. Whatever they did had to be done in great secrecy. Those considerate kings, Kamehamehas III. and IV. gave no encouragement to idolatry. They kept it down and out of sight. In the keeping of order in the parishes and in the restraining of evil practices, their vast power was felt from one end of the group to the other.

It was not so with Kamehameha V. Though in many ways a strong ruler, he was apparently without religious feeling, and heathen at heart. Under his patronage the kahuna and the hula master began very soon to operate. I well remember the revival of these things in my father's parish. The time was in the premiership and afterwards during the reign of Kamehameha V.

Even before the missionary fathers had withdrawn from the full charge of the work they began to note indications of a change. There were marked signs that a reaction had set in. The evil influence at first wrought very secretly, and the missionary did not understand it. As one said, in speaking of a certain region: "I do not understand the people of this district. There seems to be a malign influence operating among them."

Afterwards, when the missionary father had passed away, the native pastor who succeeded him, found in that fishing village, set up on one of its points of land, out of sight among the rocks, a large coral boulder, looking off to sea, which was being worshipped as the fishermen's god.

This famous stone, "Kaneaukai," is still worshipped. Twice have I helped topple it over, and once, I am told, it was toppled over by students of the Kamehameha school, and as often has it been set up again.

As one of the pastors said to me : " The superstitious element was in the makeup of the people, and
required only the opportunity for it to become open
idolatry. But while the good kings reigned and the
chiefs were alive it was easily suppressed."

It was when these restraining influences were taken
away, and in their place came rulers whose policy it
was to strengthen the royal prerogative by the encouragement of the old superstitious practices, that the
force of the idolatrous spirit began to be seriously
felt. In the days of Kalakaua it achieved its fullest
strength. In the establishment of his " Halenaua "
society, and by his other numerous heathenish practices, he fairly organized the reactionary party with all
its heathen tendencies, till, in the words of one who,
as a pastor, had felt the royal power, " Kalakaua all
but came to the act of proclaiming the abominations
of the 'Halenaua' as the religion of the land, and
himself its high priest."

It was during such days as these that the experiment of a native ministry was tried—days when fierce,
malignant influences were let loose upon the Christian
community. The native Christian worker had to meet
the old hereditary foe toward which he cherished a
certain timidity. As one remarked : " He did not love
this power of the old life. He hated it. But it was
inbred, and as it sprang again to control we felt weak
before it."

Now that we know the story so fully, it is pathetic
to go back to those bitter days and review the fierce
trials through which those pastors passed. Fostered
by the highest ruler of the land and carried on in his
very court, idolatrous practices became very general.
The white community knew little of it, but there was
not a native village, and hardly a hamlet or house,
where the kahuna did not attempt his operations or
seek some kind of recognition. They crept into the
fold of the church and corrupted its membership.

The native pastor found it impossible to turn back
the rising tide of heathenism. That which had been
an occult force, working in the darkness, at last, under
the sanction of the court, began to dare the light. It
was such a power as this that every pastor was forced
to meet and have dealings with in all the operations of
life. It invaded the sanctity of his home as well as
of his church.

As one said : " One day I lay in my house sick and
in great pain. Friends came about me and begged
me to employ a kahuna. I sturdily refused, but my
wife was prevailed upon to let him in. When I saw
him I rolled over with great effort, grasped my walking stick and struck at him and told him to be gone."

Is it wonder that some of the native pastors weakened under the spell of this malign influence, and
suffered it for a season to affect their lives ? Consider
the serious difficulty of the situation— the often help-
lessness of their sick— the real virtue of some of the
native medicines used by the kahunas and associated
with their incantations. And withal it was a battle
they had to fight out by themselves, and we so little
aware of what it all meant.

It is perhaps not enough to refer the evils of those
days solely to the revival of kahunaism. Kahunaism
was one of the most prominent features which marked
the depravity of the times   The political methods of
the day were very corrupting to the people. Kalakaua
used all the power of his vast patronage to efface pure
government. Where he dared he left no department
untouched. None but the strongest dared resist his
will. He yielded himself to the most infamous
schemes. No trust, however sacred, was above the
reach of his wicked solicitations   Officers of the
church as well as officers of the state felt the oppres-
sion of his power. Thus the national life was
corrupted. Though in his day and by his approval
many enactments were passed advantageous to the

material well-being of the land, though he was too wise to put himself in opposition to commercial interests, yet there was nothing which he thought it safe for him to do which he was not willing to do in violation of every holy law. There was to him no sacred thing but his own inordinate lust of power and self-gratification, and to its shrine he summoned the kahuna, the hula master, and all that was dark in Hawaiian character. Thus from its central seat of influence was the national life corrupted.

The wonder is that the native ministry came out of the trying ordeal, if not quite whole, yet with integrity enough left to recover so quickly from their wounds.

Again, it must not be forgotten that during this later history of the Hawaiian mission, while our native pastors were in the field suffering such disasters from the corruption of the government, and especially from the re-awakening of the old fetish worship, they had also to reckon with the Asiatic influence which came in during their day with a flood. While there were economic reasons for the introduction of Asiatic labor into these islands, while good is coming of it to the new settlers and their employers, while it is plain that lands which had been left to waste needed the tilling of industrious hands, yet the harm of it that has come to the Hawaiian people can never be told. Perhaps it was their fault, yet it was their fate to receive sore wounds.

In 1865, when the plan of putting native pastors to the front had just been inaugurated, there were 1200 Asiatics in the land; twelve years later there were 6000; eighteen years later there were 18,000; now, thirty years later, there are 39,000 The Hawaiian people could not adjust themselves to this sudden and great incursion of a new and untrained element. The Asiatics came with their faults and vices. They were thrifty, and yet they were mostly pagan. Few, if any, of them had families, and they became parasites to the Hawaiian family life. Their influence was simply more than the morality of the native people could bear. The presence of such [a horde, almost entirely without family life, worked directly to encourage prostitution and gambling and drunkenness and the opium habit.

And the Chinese, as soon as they were loosed from their contracts, began to set up for themselves. They took the native homesteads on rental, and made it possible for many natives to live without work. The thrift which has made the land to smile again with productiveness has so far mostly encouraged the easy-going, unambitious portion of the native community to live without labor.

If this is the way things must go in the meeting of the races, the stronger not only grafting their vices on the weaker, but by their very virtues putting the weaker at a disadvantage, it is unfortunate, and it accounts in part for the present state of affairs in the native community. It helps explain the present weakness of their Christianity.

Now, add to the balefulness of this mighty power of evil that has come in these later years from the Orient, a like ruin visited upon the native people by the presence of corrupt elements from Christian countries, and we may fairly conclude that it would have been most remarkable had not the native Christianity appeared just at that time so battered and weak.

During the last twenty years the power of the saloon has been felt as never before. It is now at the fullness of its strength, bringing destruction to the native race. It is an institution for which our civilization is responsible.

The evil influences represented by the corrupt white man have greatly increased during the last thirty years, and are perhaps tenfold stronger now than they used to be in the days of the missionary fathers.

We mention one more disturbing fact. It is within

these later years of the experiment of a native pastorate that the school system has been so greatly
changed. In place of being taught in their own
tongue, native children are now schooled in English.
In this way the hold of the native Christian teacher
has been weakened, and for a time the general tone of
thought lowered. The lines along which the thought
of the people had been set working with such activity
by the missionary fathers have, as it were, been thrown
out of gear. The enrire machinery of thought has
been changed. New adjustments are being made,
which in the end will doubtless result in great advan-
tage. But meanwhile, till they are achieved, the
situation has been marked by a decided weakening of
native Christian thought.

Such facts as these explain the present condition of
the pastors and the extremity to which the native
pastors have been pushed.

As we thus look back over the story of the last
thirty years, and feel the gloom of the shadows that
have rested so heavily on the native churches, we find
relief in the thought that the situation is mending.
Though the chiefs are no more, there has been raised
up a select body of educated, capable, Christian native
workers, who are devoted to their people. They will
never again lose heart in the presence of any kahuna
power, for they have dared at last to grapple with it
and try to throw it. Their costly emancipation from
it has been won.

Moreover, the power of this old heathen influence
has been broken—broken never again to rise. We
walk no longer under its baleful shadow. As an
organized power it has ceased to menace us and insult
and shame our national and social life. The seat of
our government can never again be the center of its
wicked and abominable operations. We are rid of the
hateful insults it once heaped upon us. There has
come in these last years no greater blessing to the

native churches than the revolution of January 17, 1893. It was a reformation as much needed by the church as by the state.

The influence of the Asiatic civilization is still great, but we are working to make it Christian.

The saloon remains and the many corrupt influences of the Anglo-Saxon and Latin civilizations, but there have also come with them those saving elements that are destined to overpower the evil. The influence of the foreigner is not all bad, or the native population would by this time have been swept entirely away.

The American missionary no longer fills the native pastorate, but American Christianity is getting a firmer hold of the native ministry, and, as we believe, of the minds of the more intelligent of the native community. Though undoubtedly our mission work suffered much by the change that was made in the system of education, yet, now that that change has been effected, we may look to the vast benefits to be reaped from it.

The rising generation is gaining an intelligent use of the English tongue. Stores of wealth never before brought within the reach of the native mind are thus being opened up. Heathenism can never survive the blow.

Anglo-Saxon ideas are getting control of the native mind. We need no longer fear the supremacy of Polynesian ideas Already we can predict the death of kahunaism. The native pastorate, with perhaps a single exception or two, present a solid front against it, and they are hard at work trying to release the minds of their people from its hateful power. They look back to the faultful past with shamefacedness and sorrow, but forward with hope.

CONSTITUTION AND BY-LAWS.

PREAMBLE.

We, the children of the American Protestant Mission to the Hawaiian Islands, desiring to promote the cause of Gospel Missions, as well as to strengthen the bonds of union that naturally exist amongst us, do hereby organize ourselves into a Social Missionary Society, under the following Constitution and By-laws:

CONSTITUTION.

ARTICLE 1. This Society shall be called "The HAWAIIAN MISSION CHILDREN'S SOCIETY."

ART. 2. The design of the Society is to cherish and promote union amongst its members, to cultivate in them an active missionary spirit, stir them up to good work, and more specially to assist in the support of Christian Missions.

ART. 3. The officers of the Society shall be a President, Vice-President, Recording Secretary, a Home and a Foreign Corresponding Secretary, and Treasurer, all of whom shall be elected by ballot at the annual meeting of the Society, to hold office for one year.

ART. 4. No one is eligible to fill the office of President for two consecutive years.

ART. 5. At each annual meeting of the Society, two members shall be chosen by ballot, who together with the officers mentioned in Article 3, and such members as may be chosen by the Auxiliary Societies in accordance with Article 9, shall constitute a Board of Managers, and who shall hold office for one year.

Art. 6. Any descendant of those who are, or have been members of the American Protestant Mission to these Islands, and the descendants of all those admitted into the Society in accordance with Article 7, are entitled to join the Society by paying into the Treasury the sum of one dollar annually, which shall constitute one an Annual Member, or paying at any one time the sum of ten dollars, which shall constitute one a Life Member.

Art. 7. Any other persons in active sympathy, with the object and aims of the Society may become members by recommendation of the Board of Managers, approved by a two-thirds vote of the members present at any regular meeting of the Society on payment of fees as in Article 6.

Art. 8. Any number of Life Members, resident elsewhere than in Honolulu, pledging not less than $25 annually to the Treasurer of this Society, may form an " Auxiliary " (to consist of Annual and Life Members of the Society) by the appointment of such officers, and the making of such regulations as they may wish; provided, however, all be done in conformity with Article 2 of the Constitution.

Art. 9. Any Auxiliary Society, pledging not less than $100 per annum, shall be entitled to elect annually one member of the Board of Managers of the Parent Society, to hold office one year from its annual meeting.

Art. 10. All members of the American Protestant Mission are *ex-officio* Honorary Members of this Society. Any person may be admitted as an Honorary Member of this Society by the consent of a majority of the Board of Managers, approved by a two-thirds vote of the members present at any regular meeting of the Society.

Art. 11. Any member may appeal from any action of the Board of Managers, to the Society, at any regular meeting. If the appeal is seconded, such action may be reversed by a majority vote of the members present.

ART. 12.   The Society shall hold a regular meeting on such a Saturday evening of each month as it may approve, and an annual meeting in May or June.*

ART. 13.   Each member shall receive a certificate of membership in the following form, to be signed by the President and countersigned by the Treasurer.

| Charity suffereth long and is kind; not easily provoked, and thinketh no evil.—Cor. xiii:4, 5. | Behold how good and how pleasant it is for brothers to dwell together in unity.—Ps. cxxiii:1.

This may Certify that

- -
Having paid the sum of......Dollars into the Treasury, is a ....Member of the **Hawaiian Mission Children's Society.** HONOLULU.................18..
[Signed.]   ....
                                             President.
....
Treasurer.

Go ye into all the world and preach the Gospel to every creature —Mark xvi:15. | One generation passeth away and another cometh but the earth abideth forever.—Eccl. i:4. |

ART. 14.   Alterations in, or additions to, this Constitution may be made at the annual meeting by a vote of three-fourths of the members present, such alterations or additions having been handed in in writing, at the previous meeting of the Board of Managers by any member of the Society.

---

* By resolution of the Society the time for the Regular Monthly Meetings is fixed on the Saturday immediately preceding the fulling of the moon.

BY-LAWS.

ARTICLE I.—OF THE OFFICERS.

SECTION 1. The President shall preside over the meetings of the Society, deliver an address before the Society at its annual meeting, upon vacating his office ; appoint all committees not otherwise provided for; sign all certificates of membership, arrange the programme of exercises for each regular meeting, consulting with the chairmen of the various committees, and he may convene the Society to special meetings at his discretion. He shall also be *ex officio* President of the Board of Managers.

SEC. 2. The Vice-President shall audit the Annual Report of the Treasurer ; and perform all the duties of the President in case of his absence.

SEC. 3. It shall be the duty of the Recording Secretary to keep a record of the proceedings of the Society at its several meetings, and make out an abstract report of the proceedings of the Society, during his term of office, at its annual meeting. He shall also be *ex officio* Secretary of the Board of Managers, and shall furnish the Treasurer with a certified copy of every order on the Treasurer authorized by the Board.

SEC. 4. The Corresponding Secretaries shall carry on the correspondence of the Society at home and abroad ; take charge of the books and papers of the Society, excepting the files of the *Maile Wreath*, and report at its annual meeting.

SEC. 5. The Treasurer shall receive and safely keep all moneys belonging to the Society, pay over such moneys as may be directed from time to time by the Board of Managers, for the purpose of defraying such expenses as shall have been incurred by their order, such order having the signature of the Recording Secretary; shall countersign all certificates of membership; and shall, at the annual meeting of the Society, present an accurate statement of the receipts and disbursements of the Society during the year.

ARTICLE II.—OF THE BOARD OF MANAGERS.

SEC. 1. It shall be the duty of the Board of Managers to superintend all business transactions of the Society not otherwise provided for in the Constitution, and to keep full and correct minutes of all its own proceedings.

SEC. 2. Any member of the Society desiring to bring any business before the Board of Managers, shall make known such business in a written application to some member of the Board, who shall lay it before the Board for their action thereon.

SEC. 3. The Board shall decide upon all applications for membership under Articles 7 and 10 of the Constitution; and also upon the disposition of the funds of the Society.

SEC. 4. The minutes of the Board shall be read before the Society at each regular meeting for acceptance and adoption.

SEC. 5. Any vacancies occurring in the Board of Managers, by death or otherwise, shall be refilled by regular election of the Society at the earliest succeeding meeting.

SEC. 6. The regular meetings of the Board shall be held at such times as the Board may determine, within seven days immediately preceding the regular meeting of the Society. The Secretary of the Board shall note the members present at each meeting.

SEC. 7. Special meetings of the Board may be called by the President at his discretion, or by three members thereof.

ARTICLE III.—DUTIES OF MEMBERS.

The members of the Society are expected to attend the regular meetings of the Society, as far as may be possible ; to perform all such duties as may from time to time be assigned to them ; to collect all information that may be useful or interesting to the Society, and at each regular meeting to contribute to the funds of the Society, according to their generosity and means.

ARTICLE IV.—OF MEETINGS.

The regular monthly meetings of the Society shall be opened by prayer and singing ; the minutes of the last meeting shall be read by the Recording Secretary; the minutes of the Board of Managers shall then be read and acted upon ; a collection shall be taken up by the Treasurer ; the entertainment provided for in Article 5 shall then be in order ; next shall follow miscellaneous business ; after which the meeting shall be closed by singing.

The monthly meetings of the Society shall be open to such guests as any of the members may invite as being in sympathy with the Society and its objects.

ARTICLE V.—STANDING COMMITTEES.

There shall be a committee of one on music, who shall be chosen quarterly, to aid in providing for the profitable entertainment of each monthly meeting.*

There shall be a committee of four, consisting of two ladies and two gentlemen, to be elected every four months, to conduct a monthly paper, the purposes of

---

* By resolution of the Society, the President, with two elective members of the Board of Managers, shall constitute a committee on entertainment, whose duty it shall be to secure additional attractions for our regular meetings, especially in the line of addresses or lectures.

which shall be to develop more fully the intellectual resources of the Society, and add to the Missionary interest of each monthly meeting.

There shall be a committee of one, to be appointed annually, whose duty it shall be to provide the editors of the *Maile Wreath* with suitable stationery, and to be responsible for the safe keeping of the file of the *Maile Wreath*.

ARTICLE VI.—RULES OF ORDER.

SEC. 1. In Miscellaneous business, no one shall speak more than five minutes at a time, without permission from the Society.

SEC. 2. In all points of order, the presiding officer shall be guided by the rules laid down in Cushing's Manual.

ARTICLE VII.

These By-Laws may be altered or annulled by a vote of two-thirds of the members present at any regular meeting, notice of each amendment having been given at the meeting next preceding.

HONORARY MEMBERS.

The officers of the H. M. C. S. who have the responsibility of preparing this list of names and addresses, particularly request all the members to assist by promptly informing the Secretaries of any change of residence or address; and if any errors are perceived in the printed report for the year, to send notice of the same.

Miss Annie Abell -	- Truk
Rev. James R Boyd, D.D. '	
Mrs. James R. Boyd*	
Rev. L M. Channon -	- Kusaie, Caroline Is
Mrs. Mary G. Channon	- " "
Miss E. T. Crosby -	, " "
Rev. E. T. Doane*	
Mrs. Sarah W. Doane*	
Mrs. Clara S. Doane -	- Elgin, Ill
Miss Jennie E. Fletcher -	- Carthage, Ill
Mrs. Rachel C. Forbes	- Montreal, Can
Miss Ida M. Foss - -	- Ruk, Mortlock Is
Mrs. Sarah L. (Smith) Garland	- Morning Star
Rev. Dr. William Goodell*	
Miss Jessie M. Hoppin	- Kusaie, Caroline Is
Rev Albert S. Houston -	- Gilman, Iowa
Mrs. Lizzie L. Houston	- " "
Miss L. M. Ingersol, M.D. -	- Escondido, Cal
Miss Rose Kinney -	- Truk, Mortlock Is
Mrs. T. W. Knight*	
Rev. Rudolph Lechler	- China
Mrs. Marie Lechler -	- "
Miss Alice Little	- Oberlin, Ohio
Rev. R. W. Logan*	
Mrs Mary E. Logan -	- Buffalo, N Y
Mrs. L. (Hemmingway) Morehouse	- LeRoy, Ill
Miss A. A. Palmer - -	- Kusaie, Caroline Is
Rev. E. M. Pease, D.D.	- Pomona, Cal
Mrs. Hattie A. Pease	- " "
Rev. Dr. Peck , - -	- New York
Rev. G. Pierson -	- Henrietta, Texas

*Deceased.

Rev. Francis M. Price - Truk
Mrs. Sarah J. Price - - "
Mrs. N. A. Pierson*
Mr. Frank E. Rand - - Marblehead, Mass
Mrs. Carrie E. Rand - . " "
Dr. Clinton F. Rife - - Rusaie
Mrs. Isadora Rife - - "
Miss L. S. Shattuck*
Rev. Alfred Snelling - - Truk, Mortlock Is
Mrs. Libbie M. Snelling - - " "
Rev. A. A. Sturges*
Mrs. Susan M. Sturges*
Rev. B. G. Snow*
Mrs. Lydia V. Snow*
Rev. A. H. Smith, D.D. - . Oakland, Cal
Mrs. E. D. Smith - - " "
Rev. H. J. Taylor - - Fidalgo City, Wash
Mrs. Julia A. Taylor*
Mrs. Jennie R Taylor*
Rev. T. J. Treiber - - Ipswich, South Dakota
Mrs. T. J. Treiber - - " " "
Rev. A. C. Walkup - - Gilbert Is
Mrs. Venie M. Walkup*
Rev. W. D. Westervelt - South Bend, Ind
Mrs. W. D. Westervelt - " "
Rev. Joel F. Whitney - Coventryville, N Y
Mrs. Louisa M. Whitney - . " "
Miss Louisa Wilson - - - Kusaie, Caroline Is

LIFE MEMBERS.

Abbott, Mrs. S. E. (Johnson) - - Petaluma, Cal
Adams, Anna H† - . - Boston, Mass
Adams, Rev J Q - - San Francisco, Cal
" Mrs Clara S - " " "
Aea, Hezekiah - - Honolulu, Oahu
" Rachel*
Aiken, Mrs Jennie (Willis) - - Fall River, Mass
Ailau, Mrs Mary (Pitman) - - Honolulu, Oahu
Alexander, W D - - " "
" Mrs A (Baldwin) - " "
" W D, jr - - " "
" Henry E M
" Mary C - " "

*Deceased. †Member of Ladies' Society of Essex Street Church, Boston.

Alexander, Agnes Baldwin -	-	Honolulu, Oahu
Alexander, Arthur C -	-	New Haven, Ct
" Mrs Mary E (Hillebrand)	-	" "
Alexander, Rev James M -	-	Oakland Cal
" Mrs M (Webster) -	-	" "
" Frank A -	-	" "
" Mary Edith	-	.. ..
" Edgar Wm	.	.. ..
" Sarah Eva	-	.. ..
Alexander, Samuel T .	-	" ..
" Mrs M E (Cooke)	-	.. ..
" Juliette -	-	" "
" Annie -	-	.. ..
" Wallace M	-	.. ..
Alexander, Mary J -	-	.. ..
Alexander, Chas H*		
" Mrs H (Thurston) -	-	Makawao, Maui
" Charles Frederick -	-	" "
" Helen Andrews -	-	" "
Alexander, Henry M	-	Anderson, Cal
" Lottie E -	-	Rome, Italy
Alexander, Mary E - -	-	San Francisco, Cal
Allen, Col. Wm F -	-	Honolulu, Oahu
" Mrs Cordelia -	-	" "
Andrews, Lorrin, jr*		
Andrews, Robert W	-	Honolnlu, Oahu
" Mrs Rosina S*		
" Robert S -	-	Punahou, Oahu
" Carl B - - _	-	" "
" Mrs Maria (Sheeley)	-	Honolulu, Oahu
Andrews, Samuel - -	-	Makua, Oahu
Andrews, William - .	-	Brooklyn, N Y
" Mrs A (Oscanyan) -	-	" "
Andrews, Samuel C. -	-	New York City
" Mabel A. -	-	" "
Andrews, Lucy C. *p*.	-	E. Orange, N. J.
" Lorrin A. -	-	Makawao, Maui.
Andrews, Dr. George P. -	-	Clifton Springs, N.Y.
" Mrs. Sarah D. -	-	" " "
" Winnifred - .	-	Honolulu, Oahu.
Appleby, Mrs Grace (Colcord) -	-	Woburn, Mass.
" Henry Colcord * -	-	" "
" Florence A.	-	" "
Appleton, Lilla E. -	-	Vermont.
Armstrong, W. N. -	-	Honolulu, Oahu.

*Deceased. *p* Photograph.

Armstrong, Mrs. M. F. (Morgan)	-	Hampton, Va.
" Matthew C.	-	" "
" Richard Baxter	-	New Haven, Conn.
Armstrong, Morgan Halani	-	Hampton, Va.
" Dorothy	-	" "
Armstrong, General Samuel C.*		
" Mrs. E. (Walker)*		
" Louisa Il.	-	
" Edith	-	
" Mrs. Mary Alice.	-	
" Margaret Marshall		
" Daniel Williams	-	" "
Armstrong, Mary J.	-	Los Gatos, Cal
" Amelia	-	San Francisco, Cal
Arundel, John T.	-	London, England
Atherton, Joseph B.	-	Honolulu, Oahu
" Mrs. J. (Cooke)	-	" "
" Benjamin H.*	-	
" Alexander M.	-	Middletown, Col
" Frank C.	-	" "
" Kate M.	-	Honolulu, Oahu
Atherton, Caroline*	-	
Atherton, Charles H.	-	" "
" Mrs. M. (Merriam)	-	
" Violet Merriam	-	" "
" Juliette Montague	-	"
" Laura Annis		"
Atwater, William O.	-	"
" Mrs. E. (Baldwin)*	-	
" Mrs. Annie E. (Benner)	-	
Atwater, Mrs. Lilian (Baldwin)	-	Haiku, Maui
Austin, Stafford L.	-	Hilo, Hawaii
" Mrs. C. H. (Clark)	-	" "
" Franklin H.	-	San Francisco, Cal
" Herbert	-	Hilo, Hawaii
" Benjamin H.*		
Banning, Frekerick*		
" Mrs. C. (Armstrong)	-	Oakland, Cal
" B. Rudolph	-	" "
" Frederick Armstrong*		
" Richard Armstrong*		
Bailey, W. H.	-	Oakland, Cal
" Mrs, Annie (Hobron)	-	" "
" Minnie Hobron	-	" "
" Wm. H. Jr.	-	" "
" James C.*		

*Deceased, ℘ Photograph.

Bailey, Charles A. - - - Anaheim, Cal
" Mrs. Jessie (Cameron) - - " "
Bailey, Edward H - - - Wailuku, Maui
" Horatio B - - Makawao, Maui
Baldwin, D. Dwight - Haiku, Maui
" Mrs. L. (Morris) - - " "
" Erdman D. - Hilo, Hawaii
" Charles W. - Haiku, Maui
" Lincoln Mansfield - - Lahaina, Maui
" Winnifred Morris - - " "
" Benjamin D - Paia, Maui
" Mary Elizabeth - - Haiku, Maui
" William A. - Makaweli, Kauai
" Nathaniel H.*
Baldwin, Charles F.*
Baldwin, Henry P. - - Haiku, Maui
" Mrs. E. (Alexander) - - " "
" Henry A. - - " "
" Maud M. - " "
" William Dwight - - Yale, New Haven
" Arthur Douglas - - " "
" Frank Fowler - - Lakeville, Ct
Baldwin, Samuel E.*
Baldwin, Willie Dane - West Groton, Mass
Barnet, Joseph - Kohala, Hawaii
Bartlett, George L. - Charleston, Mass
Bates, Dudley C - San Francisco, Cal
Beardsley, Grove S., M. D. - - U. S. N., Cruising
Beckwith, Rev. E. G. *p* - - Paia, Maui
" Mrs. C. P. (Armstrong) *p* - " "
" C. Amelia - - " "
" Rev. Frank A.*
" Mrs. Ellen W. (Holmes) - Mont Clair, N J
" Ruth Holmes - - " "
" Frank Holmes - - " "
Beckwith, George E. - - Haiku, Maui
" Mrs. H. (Goodale) - - " "
" Mary G. - - Honolulu, Oahu.
" George Edward*
" Martha W. - - Haiku, Maui
Beckwith, Maurice G. - Boston, Mass
Benfield, Marcus*
" Mrs. M. (Thurston)*
" Erick Lex*
" Lily J.*

---

*Deceased. *p* Photogaaph.

Benfield, Ida*
Bicknell, Mrs. E. (Bond) - - Honolulu, Oahu
  "   James - " "
  "   Ellen H. " "
  "   George - " "
  "   William B. - - Worcester, Mass
Bindt, Mrs. L. (Johnson)*
  "   Julia Louis.*
  "   Bertha Frances - - Honolulu, Oahu
  "   Paul R. - - - " "
  "   Ernest A. - - - California
Bingham, Rev. Hiram, D.D. - - Honolulu, Oahu
  "   Mrs. C. (Brewster) - - " "
  "   Hiram, Jr. - - Yale, New Haven
Bingham, Elisabeth K. - Honolulu, Oahu
Bishop, Rev. Sereno E. *p*. - - " "
  "   Mrs. C. (Sessions) - " "
  "   Edward F.*
Bishop, John Sessions, M. D. - - Portland, Or
  "   Mrs. Alice (Moore) - - " "
  "   Helen Cornelia " "
  "   John Egbert
Bishop, Bradley.*
Bissel, Rev. E. C. D.D.*
  "   Mrs. E. C. - - Somers, Conn
Bliss, Miss H. M. - - Pasadena, Cal
Bond, George S - - - Kohala, Hawaii
  "   E. Cornelius - - " "
  "   T. Spencer*
  "   William Lee - - West Branch, Mich
  "   Benjamin D., M.D. - - Kohala, Hawaii.
  "   Caroline S - - " "
  "   Abbie Steele *p* - Batavia, Ill
  "   Julia P - - Kohala, Hawaii
Bowen, W. A. - - Honolulu, Oahu
  "   Mrs. Emma C. - " "
  "   William Spencer - " "
  "   Mary Elizabeth Zilla - "
Brewer, Prof. Fisk P.*
  "   Mrs. J. (Richards)* - - Grinnell, Iowa
  "   Helen R. - - Sutton, Nebraska
  "   Mary E - - Sivas, Turkey
  "   Grace Lyman - Grinnell, Iowa
  "   Wm. Fisk - - " "
  "   Albert David " "

*Deceased. *p* Photograph.

Bray, Mrs. Mary E. -   - Oakland, Cal
Brewer, Margaret   -   - Honolulu, Oahu
Brown, C. A.   -   .   "   "
    "   Mrs. Irene (Ii)   "   "
    "   George Ii -   "   "
Brown, Louisa J. † *p*   -   - Boston, Mass
Brown, Mrs. M. E. (Spooner)   · Northwood Center, NH
Bruns, Meta   -   -   - Honolulu, Oahu
Butterworth, Joseph*   -
Campbell, Lizzie   -   - Honolulu, Oahu
Carpenter, Helen E.   -   West Woodstock, Conn
Carter, H. A. P. *p**
    "   Mrs. S. A. (Judd)   -   - Honolulu, Oahu
    "   Frances Isabelle *p*   -   -   "   "
    "   George R.   -   - Seattle, Wash
    "   Sybil Augusta*
    "   Cordelia Judd   - Honolulu, Oahu
    "   Joshua Dickson*
Carter, Charles L.*
    "   Mrs. Mary H. (Scott)   -   - Honolulu, Oahu
    ".   Henry A. P.   -   -   "   "
    "   Grace Stephens   -   "   "
Carter, Charlotte A. -   - Honolulu, Oahu
    "   Mary N.   -   -   ·'   "
    "   Joseph O., Jr.   "   "
    "   Sarah M.   -
Castle, C. Alfred*
    "   Mary Eloise -   - Wayville, P. Q., Canada
    "   H. Ethelwin Alfred   -   '   "'   "
Castle, W. R.   -   - Honolulu, Oahu
    "   Mrs. Ida (Lowrey)   -   "   "
    "   W. R. Jr.,   -   "   "
    "   Alfred L.   -
Castle, A. M. Beatrice
    "   George P.   -   -
    "   Mrs. Ida M. (Tenney)   -   ··
    "   Mary H.   -   -   -   ··
    "   Margaret Tenney   -
Castle, Caroline D.   -
Castle, Henry N.*
    "   Mrs Frida (Steckner)*
    "   Helen Dorothy*
    "   Mrs. Mabel R. (Wing) -   - Honolulu, Oahu
    "   Elinor Henry -   -   "   "

---

* Deceased.   *p* Photograph.   † Members of the Ladies' Society, Essex Street Church, Boston.

Castle, James B. - - - Honolulu, Oahu
" Mrs. Julia (White) - - " "
" Harold Long " "
Cathcart, Lillie - - - Kings Mt., N. C.
Chamberlain, Warren *p* - - Honolulu, Oahu
" Mrs. C. (Wright) . " "
" Allie M.*
Henry H. - " "
" Horace W. - Theo. Sem. Chicago, I
Chamberlain, Wm. W. - - Honolulu, Oahu
Chamberlaid, J. Evarts*
" Martha A. - Honolulu, Oahu
Chamberlain, Rev. J. P. - - La Crosse, Wis
" Mrs. H. (Lightby) - " "
" John Evarts - . " "
" Helen Maria - - Haiku, Maui
Chamberlain, Levi T. - Honolulu, Oahu
Chapin, Elizabeth D. *p* - - Winchester, Mass
Church E. P. *p* - - Lansing, Mich
" Mrs F. L. - - " "
Clark, Alvah K. - - Oakland, Cal
Clark, Mrs. H. E.*
" Mary H.*
" Arthur*
Clark, Chas. K - - Berkeley, Cal
" Mrs. H. (Howell) - - " "
" Fred Howell - - " "
Clark, Albert B., D. D. S. - - Chicago, Ill
" Mrs. Sarah (Hamlin) - - " "
" Katalena H. - - " "
" Caroline H. - - .. ..
" Albert B., Jr . - " "
Clark, Prof. Wm. S.*
" Mrs. H. (Richards) - - Newton, Mass
Clark, Mrs. H. M. (Gulick) - - Myazaki, Japan
" Admont Halsey - " "
Coan, T. Munson, M. D - - New York, 20 W. 14
" Harriet F. *p* - \ - Hilo, Hawaii
" Latimer *
Coan, Mrs. L. (Bingham) - - Honolulu, Oahu
Colcord, Chas. A. - - Searsport, Mass
Colcord, Mrs. Lizzie E. - - " "
Coleman, Chas. C.
" Mrs. Hattie (Castle) - Honolulu, Oahu
" C. A. Castle*

---

* Deceased. *p* Photograph.

Coleman, S. N. Castle · - - Honolulu, Oahu
Conde, Rev. Samuel Lee - - Rockford, Ill
" Pauline - - Chicago, Ill
" Charles A. - - Philadelphia, Pa
" Henry T. - - Indianapolis, Ind
" Mary*
Cooke, Joseph P.*
" Mrs. E. (Wilder) - - Oakland, Cal
" Joseph P. - - " "
" Grace M. - - " "
" William Gardner - Yale, New Haven.
" H. Ethelina - - - Oakland, Cal
Cooke, Charles M. - - Honolulu, Oahu
" Mrs. Anna C (Rice) - - " "
" Charles M., Jr. - Yale, New Haven
" Clarence H. - - " "
" Wm. Harrison*
" George P. - - Honolulu, Oahu
" Richard A. - - " "
" Alice Theodora " "
" Theodore A. - "
Cooke, A. Frank -
" Mrs. Lily (Lidgate) -
" Margaret M. -
" Juliet M. -
Cooke. Clarence W.* -
" Juliet M. - - - Minneapolis, Minn
Corbett, Mrs. Mary S, (Waterhouse) - Honolulu, Oahu
Corwin, John Howard - - N. Y. City
" Charles - - Chicago, Ill
" Cecil S - - "
" Arthur Mills - - "
Cowperwaithe, Mrs. Clara (Pierpont) - Berkeley, Cal
Cox, Mrs. Lydia S, (Bean) - - San Jose, Cal
Crawford, Mrs. H. J. (Sturges)*p* - California
Crocker, Charles W. - - Chicago, Ill
" Mary W. (Moseley(* "
" Lily Moseley - "
" Charles - - - "
Crozier, Mrs. Adelaide D. (Campbell) - ──── ────
Cruzan, Edith - - San Francisco, Cal
Cummings, Mrs. M. E. (Eckley) - Berkley, Cal
Damon, Samuel M. - - - Honolulu, Oahu
" Mrs. M. H. (Baldwin) - " "
" Samuel Ed. - - Yale, New Haven

* Deceased. *p* Photograph.

Damon, May Mills   -   -   - Honolulu, Oahu
Damon, Edward C.*
    "   Mrs. Cornelia, (Beckwith)   - Honolulu, Oahu
    "   Fred B.   -   -   -   "   "
    "   Ethel Moseley   "   "
    "   Maurice S.   -   "
    "   Willie F.   -   "
    "   Julia Mills   -
Damon, Frank W.   -
    "   Mrs. Mary (Happer)   -
Damon, W. F.*
Deacon. Henry   -   -   - Pepeekeo, Hawaii
    "   Mrs. Kate (Wetmore)   -   "   "
    "   Charles W.   -   -   "   "
    "   Clyde   -
    "   Sheldon   -   -   -   "   "
Deming, Mrs. Carrie (Rogers   -   - West Liberty, Iowa
Dibble, Seymour H.*
Dickson, Joshua G.*
    "   Mrs. L. (Judd)* p
    "   Hessie Judd p   - New York City
Dickson, Joshua Bates.   - Petaluma, Cal
Dickson, Mrs. S. (Conde)   -   - ——   —— ,
Dickey, C. H.   -   - Haiku, Maui
    "   Mrs. A. (Alexander)   -   -   "   "
Dillingham, Benjamin F.   -   - . Honolulu, Oahu
    "   Mrs. E. (Smith)   -   -   "   "
    "   Charles A.*
    "   Walter F.
    "   Alfred H.*   .   -
    "   Harold G.
    "   Marion E.
Dillingham, Charles T.*
    "   Frank T.   - Worcester, Mass
Dimond, W. H.   -   -   - San Francisco, Cal
    "   Mrs. E. (Waterhouse)*
    "   Mrs. Nellie (Gray)*
    "   Edwin R.   -   ,   \ -
    "   Eleanor Sophia   -
    "   Mary Gray   -   "   "
Dimond, Edwin Hall   - Honolulu, Oahu
Dimond, W. W.   -   -   -   "   "
    "   Mrs. Carrie (Higby)   -   "   "
Dodge, E. Stewart   -   -   "
    "   Mrs. E. S. (Boyd)*

*Deceased. p Photogaaph.

Dole, George H.   -   -   Riverside, Cal
   "   Mrs. Clara (Rowell)   -   -   "   "
   "   Walter Sanford   -   -   Cornell, Ithaca, N. Y.
   "   William Herbert   -   -   "   "
   "   Marion Foster -   -   Riverside, Cal
   "   Clara Maria   -   -   "   "
Dole, Sanford B.   -   -   Honolulu, Oahu
   "   Mrs. Anna P. (Cate)   -   -   "   "
Dole, Mary   -   -   Hallowell, Me   :
Doane, Edward W. -   -   -   Los Angeles, Cal
Drum, Mrs. M. (Pierpont)   -   -   ?
Edwards, Mrs. M. (Haven)   -   -   San Jose, Cal
Eels, James Jr.   -   -   Cincinnati, Ohio
   "   Emma L. A.   -   -   "   "
   "   Howard P.   -   "   "
   "   Emma P.   -
   "   Stillman M.   -   -   "   "
Ellis, Frances E.†   -   -   -   Boston, Mass
Ellis, Hattie*
Emerson, Samuel N.   -   -   Honolulu, Oahu
Emerson, Nathaniel B., M.D. -   -   "   "
   "   Mrs. Sarah (Pierce) M.D.   -   "   "
   "   Arthur Webster   -   -   "   "
Emerson, Justin E., M.D.   -   -   128 Henry St., Detroit
   "   Mrs. W. H. (Elliot) M.D.   -   "   "
   "   Paul Elias -   -   "   "
   "   Philip Law
   "   Ralph Pomeroy   -   -   "   "
Emerson, Joseph S -   -   Honolulu, Oahu
Emerson, Rev. Oliver P.   -   "   "
Farley, Mrs. Helen (Judd)   -   -   Auburndale, Mass
   "   Ruth   -   -   "   "
   "   Emily   -   "   "
   "   Charles Judd   -   ..
Flaxman, Margaret -   - .   -
   "   Sarah   -
Forbes, Rev. Anderson O·*
   "   Mrs. M. (Chamberlain)
   "   Maria R.   -   -·
   "   William J. -
   "   Harriet G. -
   "   Annie Isabella   -   "   " .
Forbes, Agnes Boyd   -   West Winsted, Conn
Forbes, Major William T.*

Forbes, Lieut. Theodore F. -	Fort McPherson, Ga
" Theodore Richards -	Bethlehem, Pa
Frear, Rev. Walter *p*	East Oakland, Cal
" Mrs. F. E. *p* -	" "
" Hugo P. *p* -	San Francisco, Cal
" Henrietta -	East Oakland, Cal
" Philip F. -	" "
" Caroline -	" "
Frear, Walter F. - -	Honolulu, Oahu
" Mrs. Mary Emma (Dillingham) -	" "
Fuller, Robert M. - -	Honolulu, Oahu
" Ellen E. - -	Oakland, Cal
Furneaux, Charles -	Hilo, Hawaii
Fyfe, Mrs. J.)Johnson)	Petaluma, Cal
" Pauline D.*	
" David K., Jr. -	" "
Galt, Mrs. Agnes (Carter) -	Seattle, Wash
" John Randolph -	" "
Gamwell, Mrs. E. M.*	
Gartley, Mrs. Ada (Jones) -	Des Moines, Iowa
Gay, Mrs. M. E. (Richardson)*	
Gay, Mrs. Marion E. (Rowell)	Riverside, Cal
Gilman, Mrs. Sarah - -	Honolulu, Oahu
" Carrie	" "
Gilman, Joseph A. - -	" "
" Mrs. Minnie (Brown) -	
" Joseph Atherton -	
" Cordelia A. -	" "
Goodale, Warren - -	Marlboro, Mass
" Mrs. Ellen R.*	
" Mary E. -	" "
" Charles W.	Butte City, Montana
Goodale, William - -	Papaikou, Hawaii
" Mrs. Emma (Whitney)	" "
" Catherine Warren -	" "
" David Whitney*	
Goodale, David. -	Butte City, Montana
Goodrich, Charles B.	
Green, Mrs. H. (Parker) -	Honolulu, Oahu
Green, Laura C. -	Makawao, Maui
Green, A. T. -	San Francisco, Cal
Green, Mrs. Mary (Paris) -	" "
" Green, John Paris -	" "
Green, Charles T. - -	—— ——
Green, Frank C. -	Worcester, Mass

*Deceased, *p* Photograph.

Greer, Mrs. Helen C. (Lyman)   -   Chicago, Ill
Gulick, Rev. L. H.*
    "   Mrs. L. (Lewis)*
    "   Kate*
    "   Edward L.   -   -   Lawrenceville, N. J.
    "   Pierre, J.*
Gulick, Rev. O. H.   -   -   Honolulu, Oahu
    "   Mrs. A. E. (Clark) *p*   -   -   "   "
    "   Oramel H., Jr.*
    "   Paul Adams   -   -   Oberlin, Ohio
    "   Katherine P.   -   -   Cincinnati, Ohio
Gulick, Rev. J. T.   -   -   Osaka, Japan
    "   Mrs. Emily *p* *   -   "   "
    "   Addison   -   "   "
    "   Louise
Gulick, Charles F.*
Gulick, Rev. Wm. H.   -   San Sebastian, Sp
    "   Mrs. Alice (Gordon)   -   -   "   "
    "   James Gordon   "   "
    "   Frederick Carlton   -
    "   Arthur Thomas*
    "   Bessie Marian   "   "
    "   Alice Gordon*
    "   Grace   -   -   "   "
Gulick, Theodore W.   -   -   Miyoshi, Japan
    "   Mrs. Agnes (Thomson)   -   "   "
    "   Walter Vose -   -   Chicago, Ill
    "   James   -   -   Oberlin, Ohio
Gulick, Rev. Thomas L.   -   -   Rosemont, Pa
    "   Mrs. Alice (Walbridge) *p*   -   "   "
Gulick, Julia Ann E. *p*   -   -   Kumamoto, Japan
Gulick, Rev. Sidney L.   -   "   "
    "   Cara M. (Fisher)   -   "   "
    "   Susan Fisher   -   "   "
Gulick, Luther H., Jr   -   Springfield, Mass
    "   Mrs. Lottie (Fetter)   -   -   "   "
Gulick, Charles T.   -   -   Honolulu, Oahu
    "   Mrs. C. T.   -   -   "   "
Hall, Caroline A.*
Hall, William W.   -   -   Honolulu, Oahu
    "   Mrs. E. (Van Cleve) *p*   -   -   "   "
    "   William Sibley.*
    "   Charlotte   -   -   Honolulu, Oahu
    "   Theodore Seymour   -   "   " .
    "   Edwin O., 2nd   -   "   "

---

* Deceased.   *p* Photograph.

Hall, Florence -	-	Honólulu, Oahu
" Philip Cushman -	-	" "
Hall, Mrs. Mary (Dame) -	-	New York City.
Hammond, Nettie -		Kamehameha Girls' School
Hardy, Jacob - -	-	Koloa, Kauai
" Mrs. E. (Andrews)*		
" Walter A. -	-	Hilo, Hawaii
" Mary H. -	-	Koloa, Kauai
" William -	-	San Francisco, Cal
Hartwell, A. S. - -	-	Honolulu, Oahu
" Mrs. C. E. (Smith) -	-	" "
" Mabel R. - -	-	" "
" Edith M. - -	-	" "
" Madeline -	-	" "
Hartwell, Charlotte Lee -	-	Honolulu, Oahu
" Juliette -	-	" "
" Charles A.	-	" "
" Bernice - -	-	" "
" Alice D. -	-	" "
Herring, May B.† -	-	Boston, Mass
Harvey, Mary (Tinker)	-	Buffalo, N. Y.
Harvey, Edna - -	-	Bangor, Maine
Hewett, Mrs. Emma (Martin) -	-	——— ———
Heydon, E. A.*		
Heydon Edwin.*		
" Asa T -	-	Seattle, Wash
" Mary*		
Hillebrand, Hermann*		
" Mrs. J. E. (Bishop)	-	Brooklyn, N. Y.
" Helen L. -	-	" "
Hitchcock, D. Howard	-	Honolulu, Oahu
" C. H. Wetmore -	-	Hilo, Hawaii
Hitchcock, Mrs. A. (Hardy) -	-	Honolulu, Oahu
" Margaret -	-	" "
Hitchcock, Mrs. M. T. (Castle) -	-	" "
" Mary R. - -	-	Hilo, Hawaii
" Hattie C.	-	" "
" Edward N. -	-	" "
" Eloise T. -	-	" "
" Mabel W.	-	" "
Hitchcock, Harvey Rexford -	-	Molokai
" Harvey Rexford Jr.	-	"
Hobron, Mrs Anna (Kinney) -	-	Honolulu, Oahu
Holman, Thomas S -	-	Chicago, Ill

* Deceased. ρ Photograph. † Members of Ladies' Society of Essex Street Church, Boston.

Holmes, Samuel -	-	Mont Clair, N. J
" Mrs. M. (Goodale) -	-	" "
" Samuel Judd		" "
" Mary G. -	-	" "
Holmes, David G. -	-	Mont Clair, N. J
" George Day -	-	" "
" Warren Goodale -	-	" "
Hooker, Mrs. M. V.†*p*		
Hopper, Miss S. V. -	-	Williamstown, Mass
Hosmer, Frank Alvan	-	Oahu College
" Mrs. Esther -	-	" "
Houston, John A. -	-	Gilman, Iowa
" Albert Rhea	-	" "
" Harold Danskin -	-	" "
Howard, Mrs. Hester L. (Dickson)	-	Los Angeles, Cal
Howard, Albert S. -	-	Townsend, Mass
" Mrs. Ellen (Goodale)	-	" "
" Lewis Warren -	-	" "
" David Goodale -	-	" "
Howard, W. L. -	-	Honolulu, Oahu
Hustace, Anne -	-	" "
Hyde, Rev. C. M., D.D.		" "
" Mrs. Mary (Knight) -	.	" "
" Charles K. -	-	" "
Hyde, Hon. William*		
" Mrs. William -	-	Ware, Mass
" Harriet -	-	" "
Hyde, William S. -	-	" "
" Mrs. William S.	-	" "
" Susan Belle -	-	" "
Bessie	-	" "
" Sylvia S. -	-	" "
Hyde, Henry K. -	-	" "
" Mrs. Lucy R. -	-	" "
Imhoft, Mrs. H. (Aswan) -	-	Honolulu, Oahu
Inch, Mrs. Clara M. (Dibble) -	-	Washington, D. C.
Ingraham, Lucretia F. -	-	Hunter, Green-Co., N.Y
Isenberg, Paul -	-	Germany
" Mrs. M. (Rice)*		
Isenberg, Paul R. -	-	Waialae, Oahu
Isenberg, Mrs. Beta (Glade) -	-	Germany
" J. Carl -	-	"
" H. A. -		"
" Julia P. -		

---

* Deceased.   † Members of the Ladies' Society, Essex Street Church, Boston.
p Photograph.

Isenberg, Clara   -
    "   Richard   -
    "   Paulae   -   -.   "
Isenberg, Rev. Hans -   -   - Lihue, Kauai
    "   Mrs. Dora (Isenberg)   -   "   "
Ives, Mrs. Helen (Chamberlain)   - Pecatonica, Ill
Jewett, Mrs. S. Fannie (Gulick)   - Oberlin, Ohio
Job, Mrs. Daniel O.†   -   - South Walpole, Mass
Johnson, A. Frances -   - Honolulu, Oahu
    "   Ellen A.   -   -   .   -   "   "
Johnson, Henry   -   -   - Petaluma. Cal
    "   Mrs. I. (Holden)*
Jones, P. C.   -   -   - Honolulu, Oahu
    "   Mrs. Cornelia (Hall)   -   -   ".   "
    "   Edwin Austin -   .   -   "   "
    "   Alice Hall   -   -   -   "   "
Jones, John J.   - Maui
Judd, Miss H. B.*
Judd, Helen S.   -   - Honolulu, Oahu
Judd, Charles H.*
    "   Mrs. Emily (Cutts)   -   "
    "   E. Pauahi   -   -   "   "
    "   Charles H.   -   .   -   - Kualoa, Oahu
Judd, A. Francis   -   - Honolulu, Oahu
    "   Mrs. A. H. (Boyd)   -   -   "   "
    "   Agnes Elizabeth   -.   "   ",
    "   A. Francis. Jr.   - Yale, New Haven
    "   James Robert   -   "   "
    "   Allan W. 2d -   - Honolulu, Oahu
    "   Henry Pratt   -   -   "   "
    ·"   Charles S.   -   -   "   "
    "   Sophia Boyd   ·   "
    "   Gerritt P. 2d -
    "   Lawrence McCully   -
Judd, Allan W.*
Judd, Juliet I.*
Kauhane, Mrs. Sarah (Martin)   - Kau, Hawaii
Kelley. Mrs. H. B. (Whitney) -   - Oakland, Cal
Kenyon, Mrs. M. F. -   -   - ?.
Kilborne, Mrs. Luella (Andrews) p - E. Orange, N. J.
Kimball, Mrs. M. A. (Manross)   - Orange, Mass
King, Sara -   -   -   - San Francisco, Cal
King, Mrs. Lucy (Conde)   -   - Rockford, Ill
Kinney, Henry A.* p

---

*Deceased. p Photograph. † Members of the Ladies' Society, Essex Street Church, Boston.

Kinney, Harriet S.*
Kinney, Mrs. S. (Dimond)*
"   Edward H.   -   Humbrest, Iowa
"   Mildred S.   -   -   Honolulu, Oahu
"   Henry R.*
"   Frances G.   -   -   Honolulu, Oahu
"   Jessie*
Kittredge, Dr. Charles S.   -   -   Santa Barbara, Cal
"   Mrs. M. (Chase)   -   -   "   "
"   Rose F   -   "   "
"   Maud C.   -   "   "
"   Mary Dame   -   -   "   "
Kluegel, Mrs. M. (Taylor)   -   -   Honolulu, Oahu
Knight, Miss E. B.*
Kofoid, Mrs. Prudence (Winter)   -   Ann Arbor, Mich
La Vergne, George de   -   -   Lihue, Kauai
"   Mary E. de (Rice)   -   "   "
"   Harry F. de p   "   "
"   Paul F. de p   -   ..   ..
"   Philip de   "   "
Leadingham, Rev. J.   -   -   Honolulu, Oahu
"   Mrs. Anna (Rich)   -   "   "
Lewers, William Henry   -   -   New York City
Lewis, Charles S.   -   -   -   Oakland, Cal
"   Mrs. L. (Wetmore)   -   -   "   "
Lewis, Raymond Whitin*
Leavitt, Mrs. M. C.‡   -   ..   -   Traveling
Leete, Hattie C.   -   -   -   Guilford, Conn
Little, Mrs. S. C.   -   -   -   Oberlin, Ohio
Livermore, Mrs. Helen (Eels) -   -   Oakland, Cal
Locke, Mrs. Mary A.   -   -   -   Mass
Logan, Beulah   -   -   -   Buffalo, N. Y.
"   Arthur C.   -   -   -   "   "
Lowrey, Fred J. .   -   -   -   Honolulu, Oahu
"   Mrs. C. L   -   -   -   "   "
"   Fred D.   -   -   -   "   "
"   Sherwood M.   -   -   -   ..   ..
"   Helen Storrs   -   -
"   Alan Jewett   -   -   -   "   "
Loebenstein, Mrs. E. (Hitchcock)   -   Hilo
Ludlow, Helen W.   -   -   -   Hampton, Va
Lydgate, John M.   -   -   -   Washington State
Lyman, Francis O.   -   -   Chicago, Ill
"   Mrs. C. (Dana)   "   "
"   Ruth C.*

Lyman, Dr. Henry M.	-	-	- Chicago, Ill
" Mrs. S. K. (Clark)	-	-	" "
" Mary I.	-	-	- " "
" Margaret K.	-	-	- Lake Forest Sem
" Henry M. K.*	-	-	-
Lyman, F. S.	-	-	- Hilo, Hawaii
" Mrs. I. (Chamberlain)	-	-	- " "
" Ellen G.	-	-	. " "
" F. S. jr.	-	-	- Honolulu, Oahu
" Francis A., M. D.	-	-	- Mendota, Wis
" Levi C.	-	-	- Kamehameha School
" Esther R.	-	-	- Hilo
" Earnest E	-	-	Pratt Inst., Brooklyn, L.I.
Lyman, David C.	-	-	- La Grange, Ill
" Mrs. M. (Cossitt)	-	-	" "
" D. B. 2nd.	-	-	"
" Frank C.*	-	-	
" Mary Ellen	-	-	- La Grange, Ill.
" Paul Henry	-	-	- "
Lyman, Rufus	-	-	- Kapoho, Hawaii
" Mrs. R. (Brickwood)	-	-	"
" Lilian H.*	-	-	
" Rufus A., Jr.	-	-	- Hilo, Hawaii
Lyman, Arthur B. R.*			
" Henry J.	-	-	Kapoho, Hawaii
" Richard L.	-	-	" "
" Eugene Hollis	-	-	Hilo, Hawaii
" Norman K	-	-	Kapoho, Hawaii
" David B. K.	-	-	" "
" Muriel C. H.*			
" Sarah Irene B.	-	-	Kapoho, Hawaii
" Clarence R	-	-	" "
" Albert K.	-		" "
" ...Charles B.	-		
Lyman, Ellen E.*			
Lyons, Curtis J.	-	-	Honolulu, Oahu
" Mrs. Julie E. (Vernon)	-	-	" "
" Isabella E.	-	-	" "
" Emma F.	-	-	" "
Lyons, Fidelia M.	-	-	Waimea, Hawaii
Lyons, Dr. Albert B.	-	-	Honolulu, Oahu
" Mrs. Edith (Eddy)			" "
" Edith Lucia	-		" "
" Albert E.	-	-	" "
Lyons, Elizabeth W.	-	-	Waimea, Hawaii

*Deceased.

Mackenzie, Rev. Robert	- San Francisco, Cal
." Mrs. Robert	- " "
Malone, Miss N. J. - -	- Waihee, Maui
Mann, Mrs. Sophia P. (Emerson)*	
Martin, George, M.D. -	- San Francisco, Cal
Martin, Mrs. Maria (Kekela) -	- Waiohinu, Kau
" Bella K. - -	- " "
Mahelona, Mrs. Susan (Kekela)	- Ewa, Oahu
Mahelona, Mrs. Emma (Napoleon)	- Honolulu, Oahu
McCoy, Henry J. - -	- San Francisco, Cal
McCully, Lawrence*	
McCully-Higgins, Mrs. Ellen H.	- Charleston, Maine
McCully, Alice L. -	- " "
McCully, Rev. Charles G. -	- Calais, Me.
" Mrs. Charles G. -	- " "
" Emma Lawaence -	- " "
" Mary Porter	- " "
McCully, Anna -	- Tokio, Japan
McCall, Mrs. E. (Whitney) -	- East Haddam, Conn
" Carrie E. - -	- " "
" Henrietta W.*	
McLennan, Martha	- Makawao, Maui
Mead, Geo. Herbert - -	- Chicago University
" Mrs. Helen K. (Castle) -	- " "
" Henry Albert -	- " "
Meredith, Mrs. R. R.†	- Boston, Mass
Merritt, Rev. W. C. - -	- Snohomish, Wash
" Mrs. M. D. - -	- " "
Mitchell, Mary L. - -	- Boston, Mass
Moore, Mrs. Alameda E. (Hitchcock)*	
Morris, Mrs. L. (Kinney) -	- Sonoma, Cal
Morris, Miss Minnie -	- Wailuku, Maui
Morse, Mrs. Mary M. (Chamberlain)	- Worcester, Mass
Mory, Mrs. Maria K. (Pitman) -	- Chicago, Ill
Moseley, Mrs. S. M. (Bingham)*	
" Hiram Bingham -	- Denver, Col
Neal, Robert M. D.*	
" Mrs. Florence (Andrews) p*	
Needham, Miss Hattie -	- Honolulu, Oahu
Newell, Mrs, M. (Hardy) -	- San Francisco, Cal
Nichols, C F., M. D. -	- Boston, Mass
Norton, Helen S. - -	- Howell, Mich
Nott, Mrs. M. (Andrews) -	- Hammond, La
" Annie W. - -	- San Francisco, Cal

---

* Deceased. *p* Photograph. † Members of Ladies' Society of Essex Street Church, Boston.

Nott, Sarah T. - - - Hammond, La
" Elizabeth W. - - "
" Mary Andrews - - "
Nott, Mrs. L. F. (Dickson) - - New York City
Oleson, Rev. Wm. B. - Worcester, Mass
" Charles M.*
" Edward P. - - "
" Mary Hall - - - "
" David Lyman - - ..
Page' Simon*
Palmer, Rev. Frank H. - Boston, Mass
" Mrs Lucy (White)*
" Herbert Hall - ::
" Allison Cleveland - - "
Park, Annie C. - - Bennington, Vt
Parke, Jennie S. - - Honolulu, Oahu
Parker, Rev. H. H. - - " "
Paris, Ella H. - Kona, Hawaii
" Anna - Kailua, Hawaii
Paris, John D. - - - Kona, Hawaii
" Mrs. Hannah (Johnson) - - " "
" Mary E. - - - " "
" John D., Jr - - " "
" James Robert - - " "
Parsons, Mrs. Henry M.*†
Payson, Adela M. - - San Francisco, Cal
Pease, Edmund M., Jr - Pomona, Cal
Perry, Charles F. - - Kamehameha
Pierce, Mrs. H. C. - ·· Honolulu, Oahu
Repoon, Helen C. - - Painesville, Ohio
Pierpont, Maria G. - - San Juan, Cal
Pierce, Henry A.*
Pierson, Mary - Henrietta, Texas
Pinder, Susan E. - - Honolulu, Oahu
Pitman, T. Henry*
" Benjamin F. - - Boston, Mass
Pogue, Rev. J. F.*
" Mrs. M. (Whitney)† - San Jose, Cal
" Samuel W. - - " "
" Jane K. - - " "
" Emily E. - - " "
Pogue, William F. - - Makawao, Maui
Pope, Ida M. - - Prin. Kamehameha Girls' Sch
Porter, Mrs. Lily F. (Brewer) - - Grinnell, Iowa
Potter, Susan M. - - Port Jefferson, L I

---

* Deceased. † Members of the Ladies' Society, Essex Street Church, Boston.

Pratt. Mrs. S. H. (Boyd) -	Greenbush Heights, N Y
Pratt, Amasa -	- Columbus, Ohio
" Mrs. A. -	" "
Pratt, Mrs. S. C. (Dickson) -	- Honolulu, Oahu
Pratt, Mrs. H. A. (Dickson) -	- Columbus, Ohio
Purdon, Mrs. Abbie (Tinker) -	- Titusville, Pa
Rand, Mabel -	- Northfield, Mass
Renwick, Isabella - -	- Honolulu, Oahu
Reynolds. Mrs. L. W. (Bingham)	
" Kate L. - -	- Boston, Mass
" Mary C. -	- St. Augustine, Fla
" Erskine H.	" "
Rice, William H.*	
" Mrs. Mary H. - -	- Lihue, Kauai
Rice, William H. - -	- " "
" Mrs. Mary (Waterhouse) -	- " "
" William H., Jr. - -	- " "
" Charles Atwood - -	- Punahou, Oahu
" Arthur H. -	" "
" Mary Eleanor -	" "
" Anna C. -	" "
" Harold W. -	- Lihue, Kauai
Rice, Mary S. H.*	
Rice, Rev. W. H. -	- Benton Harbor, Mich
Richards, Dr. James A.*	
Richards, Helen C.*	
Richards, Theodore - -	Prin. Kamehameha Manual
" Mrs. Mary C. (Atherton)	- Honolulu, Oahu
" Ruth - -	- " "
" Joseph Atherton -	- " "
Riemenschneider, H. - -	- Germany.
" . Mrs. E. L. (Rowell) p -	Honolulu, Oahu
Ritz, Laura A. - -	- Columbus, Ohio
Robertson. Cornelia D.	- Snohomish, Wash
Rogers, W. Harvey	- Papaikou, Hawaii
Rogers, Mrs. M. (Rowell)*	
" Kate Lincoln	- Medford, Mass
" Edmund H.	- " "
Rouse, Rev. Fred T.	- West Superior, Wis
Rowell, Willliam E. - -	- Honolulu, Oahu
" George A. - -	- Brooklyn, N. Y.
Sage, Sarah R. - -	- Ware, Mass
Sanford. Mrs. L. K. (Reynolds)	- Rutherford, N. J.
Sayford, Sam'l M. - -	Newton Corners, Mass
Schofield, Nathan -	-

* Deceased. p Photograph.

Scott, Mrs. H. A. *p* - -	- Hamilton, Ohio
Scott, Mrs. Emma (Clark)	- Hilo, Hawaii
" Irwin - -	- " "
" Margaret -	- " "
Scudder, Mrs. David C † -	- Brookline, Mass
Scudder, James M.† - -	- Boston, Mass
Searle, Susan A.† - -	- Kobe, Japan
Severance, Mrs. L. (Clark) -	- Hilo, Hawaii
" Helen - -	- " "
" Allen Parke	- Barre, Mass
Severence, Rev. C. M.	- Kyoto, Japan
Seymour, T. S. -	- Milford, Iowa
" Mrs. T. S.	- " "
Shaw, Jonathan	- Honolulu, Oahu
" Mrs. Della (Bishop) -	. " "
" Ruth Cornelia	- " "
" Jessie Cunningham -	" "
" Margaret Fenton	- " "
Shepherd, Fred D., M. D, *p* -	- Aintab, Turkey
" Mrs. Fanny (Andrews) *p* -	- " "
" Florence A. -	- " "
" Alice Claudia -	- " "
Shipman, W. H. -	- Hilo, Hawaii
" Oliver T.	- " "
Simpson, Lizzie W.	- Christianburg, Va
" Margaret D. -	- "
" Dora -	- "
Sisson, Mrs. E. (Holden)	- Hilo, Hawaii
Small, Sallie B. -	- York, Penn
Smith, A. L.*	
" Mrs. Clara (Benfield) -	- Lihue, Kauai
Smith, Emma C. -	- Koloa, Kauai
Smith, W. O. -	- Honolulu, Oahu
" Mrs. M. (Hobron)	" "
" Clarence H. -	" "
" Ethel F. -	- " "
Smith, Jared K., M.D. -	- Koloa, Kauai
Smith, Alfred H. - -	- Lihue, Kauai
" Juliette -	- Koloa, Kauai
Smith, Mrs. L. (Bates) *p* -	- San Francisco, Cal
Smith, Mrs. M. L. -	- " "
Snow, Caroline -	- Honolulu, Oahu
" Fred Galen -	" "
Snow, Ella B.	" "

Speer, John E.   -   Philadelphia, Penn
  "   James R.   -   "   "
  "   Hetty M.   -   "   "
Stangenwald, Hugo, M.D.   -   -   Honolulu, Oahu
  "   Mrs. M. C. (Dimond)*.
  "   Willie*
  "   Frank*
  "   Charlie*
  "   Mrs. Annie (Dimond)   -   Honolulu, Oahu
Stetson, Mrs. A. M.† -   -   -   Boston, Mass
Stewart, Martha W.*
  "   Harriet B.*
Stewart, C. Seaforth, Colonel Retired, U.S.A., Cooperstown, N Y
  "   Mrs. C. S.* p
  "   Charles Seymour   -   -   Cooperstown, N Y
  "   Cecil   -   -   U. S. Army
  "   Cora*
Stolz, Fred L   -   -   Kahului, Maui
Stolz, Mrs. M. A. (Rowell)   -   -   Newton, Mass
Street, Mrs. M. (Anderson)   -   -   Exeter, N H
Sturges, Ella M.*
Sturgeon, Mrs. Juliet Mary (Sturges)   -   Oakland, Cal
Sunter, Mrs. S. (Rogers)   -   -   Kona, Hawaii
Sutherland, Louis L. -   -   -   Minneapolis, Minn
  "   Mrs. C. L. (Moseley)   -   "   "
—Swanzy, Mrs. Julie (Judd)   -   -   Honolulu, Oahu
  "   Geraldine F.*
Taylor, Rev. T. E.*
  "   Mrs. P. G. (Thurston) -   -   Honolulu, Oahu
  "   George C.*
  "   Henry T.   -   -   Honolulu, Oahu
  "   James T.   -   -   Alessandro, Cal
  "   Edward S.   -   -   San Francisco, Cal
Taylor, Julia L. p   -   -   Fidalgo City, Wash
Terry, W. S.   -   -   Hilo, Hawaii
Thompson, Rev. Frank   -   Valparaiso, Chili, S A
  "   Mrs. Louise   -   "   "   "
  "   Carrie L. H.   -   -   "   "   "
  "   Maria Dorothea   -   -   "   "   "
Thompson, Mark V. C.*
Thrum, Thomas G.   -   -   Honolulu, Oahu
  "   Mrs. Anna (Brown)   -   -   "   "
Thurston, Asa G.* p
  "   Mrs. S. (Andrews)   -   -   ..   ..
  "   Robert T.* p

_____

*. Deceased.   p Photograph.   † Member of the Ladies' Society of Essex
Street Church, Boston.

Thurston, Lorrin Andrews -
" . Mrs M Clara (Shipman)*
"   Robert Shipman   -
Thurston, Rev. Thomas G *
"   Mrs. F. R.*
"   Alice*
"   Mrs. Alice (Gaskens) -   -   Taylorville, N C
"   Lucy G.
"   Asa 3rd.
Tousley, Mrs. Sophia C. (Corwin)*
Townsend, Mrs. Cora (Hitchcock)   -   Lahainaluna, Maui
Tucker, Edwin W.   -   •   -   San Francisco, Cal
"   Mrs. Jennie (Scott)   -   "   "
Tucker, Joshua D.   -   -   Honolulu. Oahu
Tufts, Mrs. Arthur W.†   -   Boston, Mass
Turner, Mrs. M. A. (Cooke)   •   -   Sydney, Australia
Turner, Charlotte L. -   •   -   Waihee, Maui
Van Cleve, Samuel H., M.D.   -   -   Minneapolis, Minn
"   Paul L.   -   -   Billings, Mont
Van Duzee, Cyrene   -   -   Salmas, Persia
Van Slyke, Lawrence Prescott -   -   Geneva, N Y
Vose, Miss Kate E.   -   -   -   Calais, Me
Walsh, E. M.   -   -   -   Oakland, Cal
"   Mrs. Julia (Beckwith)*
"   Marion B. -   -
"   Maurice E. -   -   •   "   "
Warfield, F. A.†   -   -   Boston, Mass
Waterhouse, J. T., Jr.   -   Honolulu, Oahu
"   Mrs. E. (Pinder) •   -   "   "
Waterhouse, Fred. T.   -   Honolulu, Oahu
"   Earnest C.   -   New York City
Waterhouse, Henry   -   -   Honolulu, Oahu
"   Mrs. J. (Dimond)   -   "   "
"   Henry, Jr.   -   -   Princeton, N. J.
"   Frank*
"   Alfred   -   -   Honolulu, Oahu
Waterhouse, William -   -   Cedar Rapids, Iowa
"   Mrs. Lena (Smith) -   "   "   "
"   Alfred Herbert -   -   "   "   "
"   Lawrence H.   -   -   "   "   "
"   Paul Bernard -   -   "   "   "
"   Gerald C.   -   •   "   "   "
"   Milicent   -   -   "   "   "   •
Waters, Mrs. Sarah E. (Coan)   -   New York City

Weaver, Phillip L.	- -	- San Francisco, Cal
" Mrs. E. A. (Armstrong)	- -	- " "
" Clarice C.	-	- " "
Weedon, Walter C. *p*		- Honolulu, Oahu
West, Alice	-	- Hilo, Hawaii
Wetmore, Charles H., Jr.*		
" Frances, M. D.	-	- Hilo, Hawaii
Wetmore, Charles		-
White, Mrs. S. (Hall)* *p*		
White, E. Oscar	-	- Honolulu, Oahu
" Mrs. Ella (Street)*		
" Clifford F.	-	- Honolulu, Oahu
White, Nellie M.	-	- " "
Whitman, Russell	-	- Oakland, Cal
Whitney, Rev. Samuel W.	-	- Ashfield, Mass
Whitney, Henry M. *p*		- Honolulu, Oahu
" Mrs. C. (Marsh)	-	- " "
" Hervey E.*		
" Henry M., Jr.,		
" James N.*		
" Albert L.*		
" Frederick D.		' Oakland, Cal
Whitney, John M., D.D.S.*p*	-	- Honolulu, Oahu
" Mrs. M. (Rice)	-	- " "
" William L.	-	- Oberlin. Ohio
" Ada Rice	-	- ' Honolulu, Oahu
Whitney, John Russell		St. Johnsburg Academy
" Edward Fisk	-	- Coventryville, N. Y.
Wight, Mrs. Laura (Wilder)	- '	- Honolulu, Oahu
Wilcox, Charles H.*		
" Mrs. Adelia (Van Meter)		- Oroville, Cal
" Ella L.	- -	- " "
" Lucy Eliza	-	- " "
" Charles H., Jr.		- " "
" Norton, Edward		- " "
Wilcox, George N.	-	- Lihue, Kauai
Wilcox, Albert S.	-	- Lihue, Kauai
Wilcox, Samuel W.	- -	- " "
" Mrs. E. (Lyman)	-	- " "
" Ralph Lyman		- Punahou, Oahu
" Lucy Etta	-	- " "
" Elsie Hart	- -	- " "
" Charles H.	-	- Lihue, Kauai
" Gaylord P.	-	- " "
" Mabel I.	-	- " "

---

* Deceased. *p* Photograph-

Wilcox, Edward P. - -	- West Winsted, Conn
" Mrs. W. (Rockwe'l) -	- " "
Wilcox, Luther -	- Honolulu, Oahu
" Clarence S.*	
Wilcox, Henry H. - -	- Lihue, Kauai
" Mrs. Mary T. (Green) -	- " "
Wilder, Mrs. E. K. (Judd) -	- Honolulu, Oahu
" William C.*	
" Gerritt P. - -	- Kahului, Maui
" Samuel G. Jr.	- Honolulu, Oahu
" James H. -	- Travelling
" Helen Kinau -	- Honolulu, Oahu
Wilkinson, Mrs. Arthur † -	- Cambridge, Mass
Williams, George C *	
Williams, Mrs. E. (Castle) -	Wayville, P. Q., Canada
Williston, Levi Lyman	- Cambridge, Mass
" Mrs A. (Gale)	- " "
Wing, Miss Grace Lilian	- Chicago, Ill
Winnie, Mrs. L. (Taylor) -	- Redwood City, Cal
Wood, Arthur B. - -	- Honolulu, Oahu
" Mrs. Eleanor (Waterhouse)	- " "
Woodward, Mrs. L. (Frear) -	- Santa Rosa, Cal
Wolfe, Mrs. N. (Goodale) -	- Honolulu, Oahu

* Deceased.   † Members of the Ladies' Society, Essex Street Church, Boston.

ANNUAL MEMBERS.

Mr. W. E. Beckwith - -	- Oahu College
Miss S. Brown -	- Honolulu, Oahu
Mr. A. W. Crocket -	-
Rev. K. J. Duncan -	- " "
Miss Florence A. Perrott -	- Ohio
Miss Laura Pires -	- Honolulu, Oahu
Rev. A. V. Soares -	- " "
Mrs. A. V. Soares -	" "

HONORARY MEMBERS OF THE HAWAIIAN
MISSION.

[EXPLANATORY NOTE.—At the May meeting of the Society, 1874, it was voted "That the Society admit by a single vote, as honorary members, all the surviving fathers and mothers of this Mission, and likewise place upon this list the names of those who have departed this life, and that in the Catalogue, the date of their arrival in this country, and of the decease of those not living, be noted." This list is printed every five years. Our last was in 1890. *The star indicates that the date of decease is not known.]

NAME.	Arriv'd	Left	Deceased.
Rev. William P. Alexander - -	1832		Aug. 13, 1884
Mrs. Mary A. Alexander - -	1832		June 29, 1888
Rev. Lorrin Andrews - - -	1828		Sept. 29, 1868
Mrs. Mary A. Andrews - - -	1828		March 10, 1879
Seth L. Andrews, M.D.† - -	1837	1849	Feb. 17, 1892
Mrs. Parnelly P. Andrews - -	1837		Sept. 29, 1846
Rev. Claudius B. Andrews - -	1844		April 4, 1879
Mrs. Ann S. Andrews - - -	1852		Jan. 27, 1862
Mrs, Samantha Andrews - -	1863	1879	
Rev. Richard Armstrong -	1832		Sept. 23, 1860
Mrs. Clarissa C. Armstrong -	1832	1880	July 20, 1891
Mr. Edward Bailey - - -	1837		
Mrs. Caroline H. Bailey - -	1837		June 11, 1894
Rev. Dwight Baldwin - - -	1831		Jan. 3, 1886
Mrs. Charlotte F. Baldwin - -	1831		Oct. 3, 1873
Rev. William O. Baldwin - -	1855	1860	
Mrs. Mary P. Baldwin - -	1855	1860	
Rev. Hiram Bingham†† - -	1820	1840	Nov. 11, 1860
Mrs. Sybil M. Bingham - -	1820	1840	Feb. 27, 1848
Rev. Artemas Bishop - - -	1823		Dec. 18, 1872
Mrs. Elizabeth E. Bishop - -	1823		Feb. 28, 1828
Mrs. Delia S. Bishop - - -	1828		April 13, 1875
Abraham Blatchley, M.D. - -	1823	1826	1860
Mrs. Jemima Blatchley - -	1823	1826	

† Married again in the United States—name unknown.
†† Married Miss N. E. Morse, New Haven, Conn. Mrs. N. Bingham died August 31, 1873.

NAME	Arriv'd	Left	Deceased
Rev. Isaac Bliss - - - -	1837	1841	1851
Mrs. Emily C. Bliss - - -	1837	1841	186.
Rev. Elias Bond - - -	1841		/
Mrs. Ellen E. Bond - - -	1841		May 12, 1881
Miss Lydia Brown - - -	1835		Nov. 10, 1869
Samuel N. Castle - - -	1837		July 14, 1894
Mrs. Angeline L. Castle - -	1837		March 5, 1841
Mrs. Mary A. Castle - -	1843		
Daniel Chamberlain - - -	1820	1823	1881
Mrs Jerusha Chamberlain - -	1820	1823	June 27, 1879
Levi Chamberlain - - - -	1823		July 29, 1849
Mrs. Maria P. Chamberlain - -	1828		Ian. 19, 1880
Alonzo Chapin, M.D. - -	1832	1835	Dec. 25, 1876
Mrs. Mary A. T. Chapin - -	1832	1835	Oct. 26, 1885
Rev. Ephraim W. Clark - -	1828	1864	July 16, 1878
Mrs. Mary K. Clark - - -	1828		Aug. 14, 1857
Mrs Sarah H. Clark - - -	1859	1864	*
Rev. Titus Coan† - - -	1835		Dec, 1, 1882
Mrs. Fldelia C. Coan - -	1835		Sept. 29, 1872
Rev. Daniel D. Conde†† - -	1837	1855	
Mrs. Andelusia L. Conde - -	1837		March 30, 1855
Amos S. Cooke - - - -	1837		March 20, 1871
Mrs. Juliette M. Cooke - -	1837		
Rev. S. C. Damon‡ - -	1842		Feb. 7, 1885
Mrs. Julia M. Damon - -	1842		June 19, 1890
Rev. Sheldon Dibble - - -	1831		Jan. 21, 1845
Mrs. Maria T. Dibble - -	1831		Feb. 20, 1837
Mrs. Antoinette Dibble - - -	1840	1845	
Rev. John Diell‡ - -	1833	1840	June 18, 1841
Mrs. Caroline P Diell - - -	1833	1840	
Henry Dimond - - -	1835		Jan. 3, 1895
Mrs. Ann M. Dimond - -	1835		Nov. 20, 1894
Rev. Daniel Dole‡‡ - -	1841		Aug. 26, 1878
Mrs. Emily H. Dole - - -	1841		April 27. 1844
Rev. Samuel G. Dwight** -	1848	*	
Rev. William Ellis ¶ - - -	1823	1824	June 9, 1872
Mrs. Mary Ellis - - - -	1823	1824	Jan. 11, 1835
Rev. John S. Emerson - -	1832		March 28, 1867

† Miss Lydia Bingbam, married October 1873.
†† Married again in the United States—name unknown.
‡ Of the Seaman's Friend Society.
‡‡ See name of Mrs. C. C. Knapp.
¶ Of the London Missionary Society.   Married again—Miss Sarah Stickney.
Mrs. S. E. Ellis died June 16, 1872.   ** Released 1854.

NAME	Arriv'd	Left	Deceased
Mrs. Ursula S. N. Emerson - -	1832		Nov. 24, 1888
Rev. James Ely - - -	1823	1828	Jan. 20, 1890
Mrs. Louisa S. Ely -. - -	1823	1828	1849
Rev. Cochran Forbes - - -	1832	1847	Nov. 5, 1880
Mrs Rebecca Forbes - - -	1832	1847	Jan. 16, 1878
Rev. Joseph Goodrich - -	1823	1836 *	
Mrs. Martha B. Goodrich - -	1823	1836 *	1825
Rev. Jonathan S. Green - -	1828	1842	Jan. 5, 1878
Mrs. Theodosia S. Green - -	1828		Oct 5, 1859
Mrs Asenath C. Green - -	1862		Feb. 4, 1894
Rev. Peter J. Gulick - -	1828	1874	Dec. 8, 1877
Mrs. Fanny H. Gulick - -	1828	1874	May, 1881
Edwin O. Hall† - - -	1835		Sept. 19, 1883
Mrs. Sarah L. Hall - - -	1835		Aug. 15, 1876
Rev. Harvey R. Hitchcock - -	1832		Aug. 29, 1855
Mrs. Rebecca H. Hitchcock -	1832		April 10, 1890
Thomas Holman, M. D. -	1820	1822 *	
Mrs. Lucia R. Holman - -	1820	1822	
Rev. T. Dwight Hunt†† -	1844	1848 *	
Mrs. Mary H. Hunt - - -	1844·	1848 *	1827 ?
Rev. Mark Ives - - ·-	1837	1851 *	1884
Mrs. Mary A. Ives - - -	1837	1853 *	1881
Rev. Edward Johnson - -	1837		Sept. 1, 1867
Mrs. Lois S. H. Johnson - -	1837		Jan. 17, 1891
Andrew Johnstone - - -	1831		July 10, 1859
Mrs. Rebecca Johnstone - -	1831		Oct. 5, 1879
Dr. Gerritt P. Judd - -	1828		July 12, 1873
Mrs. Laura F. Judd - - -	1828		Oct. 3, 1872
Rev. Henry Kinney - -	1848		Sept. 24, 1854
Mrs. Maria L. Kinney‡ - -	1848		March 6, 1858
Rev. Horton O. Knapp - -	1837		March 28, 1845
Mrs. Charlotte C. Knapp‡‡ -	1837	1841	July 5, 1874
Rev. Thomas Lafon, M.D.¶ -	1837	1841 *	
Mrs. Sophia L. Lafon - -	1837	*	
Edwin Locke - - -	1837		Oct. 28, 1843
Mrs. Martha L. Locke - -	1837		Oct. 8, 1842
Elisha Loomis - - -	1820	1827 *	
Mrs. Maria T. Loomis - -	1820	1827 *	
Rev. David B. Lyman - -	1832		Oct, 4, 1884
Mrs. Sarah J. Lyman - -	1832		Dec. 7, 1885

† Married again—Miss Mary Dame, of Massachusetts.
†† Married again, twice, in the United States—names unknown.
‡ Married to B. Pitman, of Hilo.
‡‡ Married to Rev. D. Dole.

Lightning Source UK Ltd.
Milton Keynes UK
UKHW011805021118
331648UK00012B/1933/P